A FIRST
EXISTENTIA  _NOMENOLOGY

A FIRST
INTRODUCTION TO
EXISTENTIAL
PHENOMENOLOGY

by
William A. Luijpen
and
Henry J. Koren

Duquesne University Press, Pittsburgh

Published in the United States of America
by Duquesne University Press
600 Forbes Avenue, Pittsburgh, Pennsylvania, 15282

Library of Congress Catalog Number: 79-75975
ISBN: 0-8207-0110-6
ISBN-13: 978-0-8207-0110-3

Printed on acid-free paper.

Sixteenth Printing, January 2010.

Preface

The first American edition of Dr. Luijpen's work EXISTENTIAL PHENOMENOLOGY appeared in 1960 and was reprinted for the seventh time in 1968. In spite of the fact that his treatise was not at all an easy book, it was widely adopted in many colleges and universities for both graduate and undergraduate programs. The revised edition of the same work, now published by Duquesne University Press, has been enlarged to such an extent that it may be too difficult or too long for general student use. For this reason it was decided to offer also this shorter and somewhat simplified text.

Let us add at once that this more simple version by no means removes all challenge from the book. The content has not been watered down or changed into "light reading." We think, however, that the book will prove to be both digestible and stimulating to most students.

The text closely follows that of the revised edition of EXISTENTIAL PHENOMENOLOGY, but omits certain digressions and discussions of that work. Section 8 of Chapter Two has been transferred to Chapter Five of this book, and this chapter deviates from that of EXISTENTIAL PHENOMENOLOGY insofar as it endeavors to present also a positive approach in its critique to the problem of God's existence. The extensive apparatus of footnotes has been omitted and replaced by *Suggested Readings* in English at the end of each chapter.

It is our hope that, with the increasing interest in existential-phenomenological thinking, this book may prove useful as a first introduction for undergraduate students and for non-philosophy majors in certain graduate programs.

WILLIAM A. LUIJPEN
HENRY J. KOREN

Contents

CONTENTS

CHAPTER ONE

Man as Existence

MAN has been philosophizing for more than twenty-five centuries, but the net result of his persistent efforts is a multitude of contradictory philosophical systems. While the men of positive science marvel at the astonishing fruitfulness of their own, relatively young field of learning, and pity—or mock—the poor philosopher, every century sees at least one genius come forward with a new philosophy. Man appears unable to stop philosophizing, he cannot give up philosophy. The mockers do not seem to realize that to laugh at philosophy itself is a kind of philosophy, albeit a bad kind. The funeral oration of philosophy somehow always transforms the speaker into a reincarnation of the unbeloved corpse.

Many of those whose philosophy is to reject philosophy cannot be discounted as "stupid people." Philosophy is often rejected by people who in other respects are very intelligent; they are experts in a particular branch of positive science who, precisely because of the success of their science, are tempted to absolutize the value of a special type of scientific knowledge, particularly physical science. For *this* science at least gives us "genuine and reliable knowledge."

Such an attitude, however, contains a philosophy which is in principle "complete." One who simply identifies physical science with genuine and reliable knowledge decrees that knowledge, *tout court*, is the kind of knowledge offered by physical science. But it is obviously beyond the competency of physical science to define what knowledge, *tout court*, is; that is the task of the philosopher. Moreover, one who proposes a "complete" theory of knowledge cannot avoid proposing also a "complete" theory of reality. For, no matter how he wishes to define knowledge, he cannot escape from admitting that knowledge, unlike dreaming, is a disclosure of reality. Thus, by absolutizing physical science, he proposes as a "complete" theory of reality that whatever cannot be disclosed by science is simply not real. Again, however, it is not the task of the physicist to define what reality, *tout court*, is; that task belongs to the philosopher.

Scientism is the name given to the absolutism of science, understood in the narrow sense of physical science, for until recently all positive sciences were defined as "still imperfect forms of physical science." But scientism is an internal contradiction. By claiming that meaningful statements are statements of physical science, it implies that other kinds of statements are nonsense. Now, this claim itself obviously is not a statement of physical science and therefore must be classified as a nonsense statement. Those who make the claim, however, imply that it is a meaningful statement; hence the contradiction.

The temptation to scepticism is very alluring to the philosopher, but he cannot reject philosophy without becoming a defender of the worst possible philosophy. If there appears to be no escape from philosophy, then man should try to execute this task to the best of his ability.

Whenever a new philosophy appears, bad or inauthentic philosophers turn to it to see whether at last this is *the* philosophy. Of course, their expectation meets with disappointment. The authentic philosopher knows better; he realizes that there never was and never will be such a thing as *the* philosophy. He is keenly aware of the fact that if *the* philosophy existed, there would no longer be any philosophers.

1. THE AUTHENTICITY OF PHILOSOPHY

There exist fully constituted philosophies, systems developed by outstanding geniuses. What else, then, would be more obvious than to conceive philosophizing as an attempt to "learn" a system? Such a suggestion, however, can only be made by people who fail to realize that the systems and theses of the great philosophers contradict one another. It would simply be impossible to know which philosophy one should "learn," for on what basis would one decide that one system is better than the others?

Philosophizing as a Personal Task

A much more serious difficulty is that even if a system did not contain any false thesis whatsoever, the authentic philosopher would have little use for it. For the truth of a system and its theses is not, or at least not yet, *his* truth; and it will never become his truth if he limits himself to learning those theses, with or without the "proofs." The truth of a system can never become a *personal* truth if the philosopher neglects *personally* to make his own, the reality expressed in the system. Authentic philosophy is an attempt to give a personal answer to a personal question through a personal struggle to remove the obstacles preventing understanding. The questions and answers of a system are impersonal and the obstacles which had to be cleared away are no longer relevant once the system has been constituted. If philosophy were merely a question of "learning" systems and theses, it would be a boring undertaking, and knowledge of it would no more contribute

11

to making man human than does the enumeration of the industrial centers of America.

Unfortunately, philosophy is often taught and studied in this way. Unsurprisingly, that kind of philosophy leaves its students dissatisfied. For if the questions and answers of a system do not become *my* questions and *my* answers, I never become *myself* as a philosopher. The whole affair is reduced to "talk" (Heidegger): the aspirant philosopher learns to "talk" as "one" talks in a certain tradition, and the object ultimately is the talk itself, rather than the understanding of reality. The end result of all this is a situation in which such a philosopher no longer knows whether he really understands something or is simply the victim of what "everybody always" says.

Philosophy as the "Speaking Word"

A constituted philosophy is a "spoken word" (Merleau-Ponty), solidified thought. This solidified thought, however, originated in the "speaking word," the personal expression of reality. If philosophy is a personal affair, a "speaking word," it can find its starting point only in my personal presence as a philosopher to reality. This presence is called "experience."

The term "experience" should be understood here in the broadest sense. There are many ways of experiencing which place us in the presence of a particular reality. There is a difference in experiencing a rock, a rose, H_2O, a liar, a board of examiners, a police officer, and being as being. They are different because they are not what they are without a determined "attitude" of the subject (Husserl). To experience the reality of a board of examiners, I must be able to place myself in the "attitude" of an examinee who can fail. An entirely different "attitude" is required to experience the reality of a rose. One who as-

sumes an esthetic "attitude" is not attuned to the reality of
an angry police officer; this reality requires that I assume
the "attitude" of an actual or possible violator of the law.
All this does not indicate when an experience must be
called philosophical, but at least this much is certain: to
be meaningful, a philosophy must give expression to reality. Thus it follows that the philosopher must start from
experience. If he were to start from theses, he would never
know what he should admit as truth. Such a "philosopher" does not *see* any reality; yet a person becomes a
philosopher only insofar as he *sees*. And seeing is something which he does either in person or not at all.
Therefore, philosophical formation cannot consist in
drilling the aspirant in certain theses. There can be an
authentic philosophical formation only insofar as the aspirant is aided to *personally* see reality. Even a real formation—that is, one which does not amount to a mental drill
for practical purposes—implies a risk of falsifying the
aspirant's philosophical activity, because in helping one to
see personally the aid consists, and has to consist, among
other things, of imparting knowledge of previously philos-
ophized philosophy. But how often does it not happen
that the program does not go beyond this point? The
greatest enemies of authentic philosophy often are the
professors of philosophy (Heidegger).

Philosophy as a Common Task

The goal of personal thinking cannot be reached independently of tradition. As a philosopher, I am a person,
and my philosophical thought is only authentic if it is *my*
thinking. But I am inserted into a history which I myself
have not made; I cannot begin to think from zero, for
others have thought before me and I am carried by their
thought. I live in the stream of thought established by

13

tradition, at least because of the language I speak and because of the ideas embodied in this language. It is impossible to think without language, and it is just as impossible to think without tradition.

It does not follow that the philosopher has to abandon any claim to personal thought. Although he is carried by the history of thought, the philosopher is called to infuse new life into this history. He does this when he makes a profound study of the philosophers of the past. They have important things to say; in their own way they gave expression to their experience of reality and set it down in their works. There they speak to us and enter into contact with us.

This contact does not mean that we are simply invited to take over their system, for such an invitation would be an attempt to seduce us into inauthenticity. The true value of the works produced by the philosophers of the past is that they try to make us sensitive to the reality which they have perceived. Philosophizing is always concerned with a *personal* experience and a *personal* expression of the wealth of being, but it is because others preceded us that we are able to *personally* see something to which otherwise we might have been blind.

If there had been no Plato, our conception of reality would have been much more trivial and materialistic, and hence our understanding of its deepest meaning would have been much more superficial. Without Augustine, we would perhaps not have been sensitive to the meaning of restlessness in our being-in-the-world. To Darwin, Marx and Freud we owe our victory over exaggerated spiritualism. The philosophers of the past speak to us to make us personally sensitive to the wealth contained in the totality of all that is.

Thus there is no reason to be scandalized by the existence of many contradictory systems. What matters it not the system but reality. And in every system some aspect of reality finds expression. Perhaps the philosopher unduly elevated this aspect of reality to the rank of reality, pure and simple, or absolutized a certain experience as the only valid one. For this reason the resulting system may be limited and antiquated, but certainly it is not without value.

Accordingly, the fact of being inserted into a history which is not of his own making does not prevent the authentic philosopher from thinking in a personal, relatively independent and autonomous fashion. This is on the condition that he take up the past in a creative way, endow it with a new life. Only *he* can do this. He does not sign a pledge of allegiance to any school of thought, but listens to reality, no matter from where it speaks to him. When he studies the works of the past, he begins with an attitude of trust in those who speak to him, because he realizes that they do not demand anything else of him than that he *himself* accept or reject their insights. For philosophy does not exist in statements and theses but in the personal expression of reality on the basis of a personal presence to reality.

The same applies to the so-called "principles of philosophy." They are not man's most general judgments but rather experience itself in its most fundamental dimension. In systematized philosophies these fundamental experiences are set down in explicit judgments. To be really meaningful, however, they must be given life again by philosophy conceived of as a "speaking word," a personal expression of reality.

"Back to reality itself" was the watchword of Edmund Husserl, the founder of phenomenology. This imperative is valid for all authentic philosophical thinking. While studying systematized philosophies, the philosopher must attempt to return to the reality intended by any statement whatsoever. Only in the presence to reality is it possible to arrive at the incontrovertible and accept it personally. Only in this way does truth really become *my* truth, and are "talk" and "ambiguity" overcome.

The Intersubjectivity of Philosophical Truth

The assertion that truth, to be authentically philosophical, must be truth-for-me can be exaggerated. Following Kierkegaard, some say that philosophical truth is *per se* not truth-for-all, not intersubjective. Thus, where philosophers reach agreement, philosophy would cease to be philosophy. Intersubjectivity would be an exclusive character of "scientific" truth.

This standpoint is now antiquated and abandoned because it contains a hidden contradiction. Anyone who seriously defends the view that truth is not truth-for-all implies that this view is true and therefore, in principle, valid for all. And if he defends it while holding that his view is not valid for all, not true for all, he is not making any statement.

It is true, of course, that it is easier intersubjectively to undertake research and verify the results in a positive science than to intersubjectively examine a philosophical question. Thus there actually exists more agreement in positive science than in philosophy. In principle, however, any truth is intersubjective because truth is truth.

The fact that truth is not recognized by all should not induce us to profess a relativistic attitude of indifference, that is, let us leave everyone his truth or error, without any attempt to arrive at mutual agreement. As a matter of fact, the essential intersubjectivity of truth reveals itself in this that it is impossible to barter with truth: if you accept part of *my* truth, I'll accept part of *yours*. Truth as truth is disowned when tolerance is interpreted as relativism.

The authentic philosopher realizes that truth has an absolute right to recognition, and this makes him to some extent intransigent. Truth is truth and therefore must be recognized as such. Anyone who wishes to do violence to truth will find the philosophers against him. In a certain sense the philosophers speak as functionaries or representatives of mankind (Husserl), they protect one of man's most precious possibilities. When a society begins to base itself upon lies, the philosophers will either fall as martyrs or begin to function as puppets, i.e., they cease to be true philosophers.

The "Usefulness" of Philosophy

In the eyes of many positive scientists philosophy is a joke, "nice poetry." In self-defense the philosopher could be tempted to demonstrate the usefulness of philosophy, but such an effort would be in vain. Those who can understand the term "useful" only as the usefulness which they experience in the pursuit of their positive science cannot see the value of philosophy. Nuclear physics, biology, economics, psychometrics and such sciences are useful, they serve the workaday world in which they are integrated, but philosophy is wholly useless with respect to this world. Philosophy is characterized by a "uselessness" which it cannot abandon under penalty of ceasing to be philosophy. But it is precisely because our society tends more and more to become a technocratic order of work and functions that philosophy is not only "useful"—albeit in a totally different sense than its technocratic meaning —but even necessary, at least for many.

This assertion cannot be proved outside the actual pur-

17

suit of philosophical thinking: understanding the usefulness and necessity of philosophy presupposes the actual
experience of philosophizing. This experience is missing
in people who are totally immersed in a technocratic mentality; hence they could at most accept in good faith what
the philosopher says about the value of philosophizing.
But such an acceptance is non-philosophical. As a rule,
therefore, the plea for the usefulness of philosophy fails to
convince the non-philosopher. Philosophers, on the other
hand, do not need such a plea, because the value of philosophy clearly reveals itself in philosophical thinking itself.

*Existentialism, Phenomenology, and Existential Phenom-
enology*

From what we have said about the authenticity of philosophy it should be evident that existential phenomenology itself may not be called *the* philosophy. Existential
phenomenology also will be transcended, for it always remains possible to express the ultimate meaning of life and
reality in a better way. Guesses, however, as to the future
philosophy are a waste of time. It will be more useful to
pay attention to the recent past of existential phenomenology, for it offers the reader a measure of historical orientation.

Soren Kierkegaard is the founder of existentialism, but
one could hardly call him a phenomenologist. Husserl
launched phenomenology, but was not an existentialist.
Thus there was a time when a distinction needed to be
made between existentialism and phenomenology. Today,
however, we also speak of existential phenomenology or
phenomenological existentialism. So the question may be
asked: what is the difference between existentialism and
phenomenology, and how did the unified movement of
existential-phenomenological thinking arise?

18

Let us point out first of all that there exists a certain harmony between Husserl and Kierkegaard. It manifests itself in their common resistance to the atomistic way of looking at man and things human. Man is not more or less like an atom. The way in which Kierkegaard and Husserl resisted that view differs: Kierkegaard speaks of man, while Husserl practically limits himself to consciousness or knowledge. Kierkegaard conceived man as "existence," as a subject-in-relationship-to-God. Man is not a self-sufficient spiritual "atom" but, as a subject, is only authentically himself in his relationship to the God of revelation. According to Kierkegaard, "existence" is absolutely original and irrepeatable, radically personal and unique. His emphasis on the uniqueness of "existence" implies that a thinker's assertions are applicable only to the thinker himself: in principle, they do not claim validity for others. Thus, Kierkegaard's position is deliberately anti-"scientific": it cannot do justice to the dimension of universality claimed by any "science" (we do not use the term here in the sense of positive science). As a matter of principle, Kierkegaard's thinking cannot go beyond the monologue, the "solitary meditation."

Kierkegaard's followers resolutely countered the reproach of being "unscientific" by saying that existentialism *may not* be a "science." Their objection to being called "scientific" appeared to be largely based on a particular sense of the term "scientific" as used with respect to man. In scientism and in the philosophy of Hegel—the black sheep in Kierkegaard's works—man was "scientifically" discussed in such a way that the original and unique character of human subjectivity simply disappeared under verbiage. Yet this kind of speaking was supposed to be "scientific" *par excellence.* The need to reject a *particular* conception of "scientific" thinking, however, does not entitle anyone to claim that philosophi-

19

cal thinking about man must not be "scientific" in any sense whatsoever. The philosopher can hardly avoid the use of universal and necessary judgments to indicate the universal and necessary structures of man. In this sense he is "scientific."

This difficulty hardly existed for Husserl. Originally a mathematician and physicist, Husserl, like Descartes, was disturbed by the confusion of language and the welter of opinions existing in philosophy. Clearly, philosophy was "not yet a science," and this made Husserl launch his phenomenology as an attempt to make philosophy also a "rigerous science." He was clever enough to avoid the trap of ascribing to philosophy the same scientific character as belongs to the positive sciences. Philosophy cannot allow physics or any other positive science to dictate its methods, for the simple reason that philosophy is not a positive science. It has to become scientific *in its own way* in its expression of intersubjective and objectively general truth.

To realize his ambitious plan, Husserl investigated man's consciousness or knowledge. He conceived consciousness as intentional, orientated to something other than itself. Whereas Husserl addressed himself to problems in the theory of knowledge, Kierkegaard tried to answer theological-anthropological questions. The distinction between existentialism and phenomenology consisted primarily in the different directions of their concern.

The two streams of thought merged in Heidegger's BEING AND TIME, where they served as the foundation of the philosophy now known as "existential phenomenology." Heidegger's philosophy of man does not lapse into the illusions of either idealism or positivism. Influenced by the phenomenological theory of knowledge, existentialism gave up its anti-scientific attitude. Phenomenology, on the other hand, enriched itself and developed into a philosophy of man by borrowing many topics from Kierkegaard's existentialism. In this way there arose the unified movement of existential-phenomenological thinking of which Heidegger, Sartre—though not in every respect—Merleau-Ponty and the Higher Institute of Philosophy of Louvain are the principal exponents.

We wish to make the reader experience the value of philosophy in a "true to life" fashion here. By making him think philosophically, it is possible to "say" what philosophy is and how valuable the philosopher's "useless" thinking is. We are convinced that philosophy is indispensable in the development of modern society with its increasingly more technocratic mentality. The more this mentality penetrates and the wider it ranges, the more difficult it also becomes for man to consent to life. But—what is man? That is the first question which imposes itself here.

2. Materialistic and Spiritualistic Monism

The lack of balance present in the materialistic and the spiritualistic views of man shows how difficult it is to express what man is. This imbalance, however, does not make these views useless, for there is no philosophy which totally failed to "see" anything. Yet, moments of equilibrium are relatively rare in the history of philosophy. Existential phenomenology presents itself as such a moment of equilibrium. Retaining the truths seen by the materialists and the spiritualists, it does not fall into the one-sidedness of either system. It is in the use of the term "existence," as expressing one of man's most fundamental characteristics, that this balanced vision of man is crystallized.

Materialism

All materialistic systems agree that man is the result of cosmic processes and forces, just as things are results of cosmic processes and forces. Thus the materialist would say that the being of man is a being-in-the-world in the sense that man is a thing among other things in the world, a moment in the endless evolution of the cosmos.

This idea cannot be dismissed as wholly foolish. It expresses a valuable vision, it takes seriously the irrefutable fact that man is whatever he is on the basis of matter. Sooner or later any philosopher must be tempted to agree with materialism if he does not wish to depreciate the importance of matter. For it is only a small step from the view that man is whatever he is on the basis of matter to the conviction that man is nothing but matter, a mere fragment of nature. After all, there is no spiritual knowledge without physiological processes, no spiritual love without sensitive love, no personal conscience without biological substructures, no artistic act without expression in matter. The biologist as a biologist can speak, for instance, about knowledge, love and conscience, and what the biologist says in these matters is not idle talk but concerned with reality.

Materialism is often camouflaged. Most of the time it parades as scientism. Esteem for the sciences becomes scientism when one asserts that there are no other realities than those disclosed by the physical sciences. Precisely because man is whatever he is only on the basis of matter, the sciences are able to say something about everything man is. In principle, for example, it is possible that there is a physiological difference between a saint and a criminal or that an operation can produce in the criminal the material conditions for a virtuous life. Many alcoholics and prostitutes are not primarily—sometimes not at all— "transgressors of moral laws" but sufferers from bodily deficiencies, for which a cure is more appropriate than is punishment. Thus it is easy to see that one can be greatly tempted to claim that the sciences are able to say all there is to say about any reality. If man is whatever he is only on the basis of matter, there is nothing about which the sciences have nothing to say. Why, then, should we not go one step further and assert that, when the sciences have spoken, there is nothing else to be said? That fatal step makes esteem for the sciences degenerate into scientism. Scientism is a materialistic theory; for its adherents there exists nothing worth mentioning apart from the material things with which the sciences are concerned.

Materialism as a "Detotalization of Reality"

Materialism fails in its attempt to express what man is because it indicates only one aspect of man, albeit an essential one. It is a "detotalization of reality" (René Le Senne), it commits the "fallacy of misplaced concreteness" (Whitehead). Materialism is a kind of monism: in the totality of reality it leaves room for only one type of being, viz., the being of the material thing. Therefore, man is simply a thing, and human life is nothing but a chain of processes.

Generally speaking, a philosophy does not fail by what it says, but by what it disregards or eliminates from reality. This principle clearly applies to materialism. The materialist disregards the fact that man exists for himself as man, that is, that being-man has *meaning* for man, and that things do not have meaning for themselves or for other things but only for man. If there were only things, nothing would have any meaning. Materialism disregards the fact that only with and through man can there be question of things and processes. Only man can say that things are and what they are, that he himself is and what he is. Man is the original sayer of "is." No matter how thinglike man may be, it will never be possible to think away the "dimension" of man which makes it possible for him to say "is" with respect to both himself and things. It is this which makes man transcend the thinglike aspect of his essence, and it is this "dimension" of man which all non-materialists call man's subjectivity.

Accordingly, it is man's subjectivity which the materialist simply disregards. He neglects an essential aspect of man's being because he fails to recognize that being-man is a being-conscious. The materialist cannot defend himself by saying that, like all material processes, man's acts of consciousness also can be reduced to an interplay of atoms. For he would have to admit that some "atoms" distinguish themselves from other atoms by existing for themselves as atoms: they can philosophize about themselves and about other atoms or formulate an atomic theory. Now, these special "atoms" we call "men."

Materialism is viable only because the contradiction it entails lies hidden. The materialist, as a materialistic philosopher, cannot account for his own being if he holds fast to the view that there exist only things. The contradiction is this: on the one hand, he admits that geological layers, rainstorms, plants and animals cannot create a philosophy, not even a materialistic philosophy; on the other, as a materialist, he wishes to explain his own being by means of the same categories through which he expresses the being of geological formations, rainstorms, plants and animals. He disregards the fact that in materialism there is not only the material world but also the materialistic philosopher. The existence and peculiar nature of the latter remain unexplained.

24

The fact that things and processes have a meaning for man as a conscious subject justifies our attributing to subjectivity a *certain* priority over things. One who thinks away the subject removes all meaning, so that the term "is" becomes meaningless. For what could "is" possibly mean if there is no subject who *affirms*, says "is"? Even the very supposition of the subject's absence can be made only in a purely verbal fashion; it cannot *really* be made. The subject, then, is beyond dispute and reveals himself endowed with a certain priority over the world of things.

Heidegger calls the aspect by which man transcends things "nothingness," that is, no-thingness, because it cannot be like the being of things explained by the sciences; the objects of the sciences do not pursue science. He calls the subject "non-being," because the subject is not like what he has called "being," the cosmic being of things. This "non-being," however, is not simply nothing but something positive, no-thing, a positivity which "lets be" the being of things.

Toward an Absolute Priority: Spiritualism

As soon as one realizes the importance of the subject, there is a danger that this importance will be exaggerated. Without the subject, the *I*, the world of things is not what it *really* is, viz., non-I. Without the *I*, the world of things cannot be spoken of and the term "is" loses all meaning. Only a slight exaggeration is needed to make one consider things the result of a kind of creative activity exercised by the subject or the content of the subject's consciousness.

Spiritualistic monism absolutizes the subject by reducing the being of material things to that of the subject. In other words, it "detotalizes" reality in exactly the opposite direction. Materialism disregards the importance of subjectivity, but spiritualistic monism lets the density of ma-

25

terial things evaporate into "thin air": they are reduced to mere contents of consciousness.

Spiritualistic monism takes seriously the subject's originality, neglected by materialism. As a subject, man cannot be merely the result of material processes; hence the subject is original. If this originality is exaggerated, however, one eliminates not only the subject's receptivity with respect to material things, but even the possibility of recognizing other subjects as subjects. For how could a self-absolutizing subject recognize and accept the fact that another subject is an *other* subject, possessing an identity of his own with respect to the self-absolutizing subject? The self-absolutizing subject cannot avoid reducing the other subject to a modification of himself. As soon, however, as the *I* conceives itself as containing all other *I*'s, it can no longer conceive itself as the "little," finite *I*, distinct from the other little *I*'s.

Spiritualistic monism, then, cannot avoid sacrificing the distinct identity of the "little" *I* to the Absolute Subject. A "great" impersonal Subject takes the place of the "little" subject who any real subject is, and the many distinct subjects are viewed as particularizations, dialectic moments or function of the impersonal Subject. The consequences of such thinking are typically illustrated by Fichte's Absolute Ego and Hegel's Absolute Spirit. The qualifications of the Absolute Subject ultimately become so fantastic that they are identical with the traditional attributes of God. Thus spiritualistic monism terminates in the deification of the subject.

In reality, however, the "little" subject is a *little* subject, one who is and remains unmistakably relative. But the Absolute Subject is assumed to think and act in and through the "little" subject. Since in reality only the "little" subject exists, the assertion that the Absolute thinks and acts through the "little" subject actually amounts to saying that the thinking and acting of the "little" subject carries the weight of the Absolute. Thus it can happen that a man thinks that he can speak with "divine" authority and act with a "divine" guarantee. He assigns to his convictions and assertions so much importance that, as a matter of principle, he cannot listen to anyone else and looks upon any attack on his "truth" as irreverent or blasphemous. He fancies that he can speak in the name of the Absolute and holds his "truth" to be God's design for the world and man, a design which gives a "divine" sanction to his actions.

In spiritualism hardly anything remains of the original inspiration which gave rise to materialism. Spiritualism simply buries under verbiage the fact that man is whatever he is only on the basis of matter.

Accordingly, there is every reason to seek an intermediary view which takes into account the valuable insights of both materialism and spiritualism, while avoiding the extremes of both. Existential phenomenology rises to this challenge. But first, however, we would like to speak of Descartes, because existential phenomenology is continually in opposition to philosophies which somehow arose from Descartes' ideas.

3. DESCARTES

At the end of his studies at the famous Jesuit College of La Flèche Descartes (1596–1650) came to the conclusion that his endeavor to acquire knowledge had given him only a clear realization of his own ignorance. He had experienced that in philosophy there was nothing at all about which philosophers did not disagree. He therefore resolved to pursue no other knowledge than that which he could find in himself and in the "great book" of the world. After spending some years in trying to acquire experience, Descartes began to investigate the *way* by which truth and certainty could be reached. He had never abandoned hope of finding this way, for he could not forget the shining example of mathematics. Starting from a few very simple axioms, mathematics analytically proceeds to unfold the theses implied in those axioms. Descartes suspected that it should be possible to build the entire edifice of human knowledge in a similar fashion and so he devoted his entire life to the construction of that "wonderful science" of a universal mathematics.

The "Cogito"

To discover the incontrovertible starting point for that wonderful science, Descartes found it necessary to use methodic doubt: anything which somehow is subject to doubt must be "bracketed," i.e., judgment is suspended with respect to it. Methodic doubt does not mean that Descartes is a sceptic or an agnostic, but wishing to find the truth and certainty of a universal mathematics, he is obliged to demolish his old opinions down to their very foundation because he has experienced how doubtful everything is that he has learned.

His methodic doubt covers everything which is not the subject himself. Descartes provisionally wishes to suspend every judgment about God, the world and the body, not because he really doubts the existence of God, the world or the body, but because everything he has learned about them still lacks a foundation, even if it is something that is true.

The reality of world and the body must be doubted because our senses are unreliable and we may be dreaming. The fact that the senses sometimes deceive us implies that they could always be deceiving us in what they tell us about the world and the body. And just as one might be convinced that his dream-body and dream-world are real, so one might be convinced that the pen or the book on the table are real. And there is no criterion by which we can determine that we do not dream when we think that we perceive a real pen, a real book and a real table. Nevertheless, when man has "bracketed" everything which is subject to doubt, the fact of his doubting itself remains indubitable and certain. His doubting thought, his *cogito* remains certain and beyond doubt. Consequently, says Descartes, it is also beyond doubt that I who think *am* something. In this way *"cogito, ergo sum,"* "I think, therefore, I am," constitutes the incontrovertible starting point of Descartes' planned "wonderful science."

Consequences of the Cogito's Primacy

Descartes' radicalism begins to show its consequences in the very first truth of his philosophy. The thinking subject, the *cogito* is beyond doubt—but, what is this subject? Descartes cannot answer: the subject is embodied or involved in the world, for the reality of the world has been "bracketed." His only possible answer to the question, What am I? can be: "I am thinking," for thinking is the only thing he has not "bracketed." Thinking *what?* Descartes cannot answer: "I am thinking of God, the world or the body," for their reality has been "bracketed." His only possible answer is: "I am thinking my own thoughts," for thinking is the only thing he has not "bracketed": I am conscious of the contents of my consciousness, and this is what I am, a thinker of thoughts.

Note that Descartes' methodic doubt does not remove God, the world and the body from his *thought*, but merely affects them with the qualifier "thought of." This qualifier gives the *cogito* its incontrovertible certainty. For, even if the pen I use and the paper on which I write are not real

29

but merely dreamt, it still remains incontrovertible that I have the pen-idea and the paper-idea. The *cogito*-with-its-contents is beyond doubt.

The Criterion of Truth and Certainty

Because his "wonderful science" would contain only truth and certainty, it was very important for Descartes to investigate why his starting point—I think, therefore I am—was so certain. He came to the conclusion that the only reason was that he *clearly* and *distinctly* saw its truth: in order to think, one must exist. Thus clarity and distinctness became for him the criterion of truth and certainty. He would ascribe truth and certainty only to things of which he had clear and distinct ideas.

But what guarantees that clear and distinct ideas can be trusted? At this stage Descartes proceeds to prove the existence of God in order to be able to affirm that those clear and distinct ideas come from the Creator: God's veracity precludes that he deceives man. God, then, guarantees the truth and reality of anything conceived in clear and distinct ideas. Our task, therefore, is to determine which ideas are clear and distinct.

Man

Only the idea of extension, Descartes holds, satisfies the criterion of clarity and distinctness with respect to matter. Whatever is material is essentially extended, quantitative, and nothing else. Now, only the physical sciences study nature by means of categories of quantity; hence affirmations which cannot be made by these sciences of nature turn out to be meaningless in the "wonderful science" which is concerned with incontrovertible certainty about truth and reality. Needless to say, this is scientism.

Descartes' standpoint is heavy with consequences for his view of man. On the one hand, man is a *res cogitans*, a thinking substance; on the other, he is also a *res extensa*, an extended substance. Because material reality is nothing but quantity for Descartes, every change has to be *per se* a spatial change. The "human" body, therefore, is nothing but "spatially moving quantity," a machine, the object of mechanics. Man, then, consists of two substances which are in principle and essentially separate and independent of each other.

Of course, it did not escape Descartes that the subject —which he called "soul"—and the body constitute a certain unity. This is obvious from our feelings of hunger and pain. When a wound hurts me, my "thinking substance" does not perceive the injury in the same way the captain notices that something is broken on his ship. Descartes is thus forced to admit that soul and body exercise a certain influence on each other. Strictly speaking, this should not be possible, but the fact cannot be denied. Descartes vainly tried to solve the difficulty by locating the soul in the pineal gland, but he himself was not very happy with this artificial solution. Its insufficiency is not surprising: Descartes was attempting to answer the question of how two substances which are *essentially not* a unity can constitute an *essential* unity.

Observations

Those who affirm the priority of the subject, we saw, run the risk of letting this correct insight degenerate in that real things are reduced to subjective contents of consciousness. Nothing then remains of the strong point of materialism, viz., that man is whatever he is only on the basis of matter. Strictly speaking, this degeneration occurred already in Descartes himself, although he managed to escape its consequences by being illogical, by filling the subject with clear and distinct ideas of the body and the world, guaranteed by God's veracity. Through this unjustifiable appeal to God, Descartes "restored" man's grip on the reality of the body and the world. His theory is a mitigated form of spiritualism and less consistent than the absolute spiritualism of Spinoza and Hegel.

Descartes, we saw, never really doubted the reality of worldly things: his methodic doubt merely attached to the body and the world the qualifier "thought of." He obviously realized that the pen I use, the paper on which I write and the chair on which I sit are something "more" than the pen-*idea*, the paper-*idea* and the chair-*idea*. But what could this "more" be? Because Descartes had reduced the *human* aspect of things, their being-for-the-subject, to a content of consciousness, this "more" could not be a being-for-the subject; it had to be "brute" reality, reality divorced from the subject. Thus the reality of things was, as it were, split into two: a human side—being-for-us—and an inhuman side—being-in-itself. The human side was located "inside" the subject, the inhuman side "outside" the subject.

The obvious question to arise here was: to what extent does the "inside" world agree with the "outside" world? Is there anything "objective" corresponding to the ideas "inside" the subject? "Objective" here refers to "brute" reality, for the subject and the world are divorced from each other; hence the world is looked upon as a collection of things-in-themselves. Descartes, we saw, thought that he could "affirm" the reality of a world-in-itself because clear and distinct ideas "inside" the mind are guaranteed by God's veracity. A world-in-itself, however, is by definition an inhuman world, a world beyond the reach of the subject, a non-affirmable world. Obviously, such a world cannot be *really* affirmed.

In spite of all these difficulties, the "spirit" of Descartes became part and parcel of philosophy; the subject was divorced from the world, and the world was put out "there" separate from the subject. By opposing this divorce, existential phenomenology also oppose itself to the "spirit" of Descartes.

4. EXISTENCE AS CONSCIOUS-BEING-IN-THE-WORLD

As was said, existential phenomenology tries to preserve the valuable insights of both materialism and spiritualism, while avoiding their exaggerations. With spiritualism it affirms that man is a subject, with materialism it affirms that man is whatever he is only on the basis of matter. The subject who man is, then, is not an Absolute Subject but an "existent" subject. Man as subject is "existence." This term is taken in a technical and literal sense: man "ex-sists," he "puts himself outside himself."

What does this "outside" of the human subject mean? Within the context of the struggle between materialism and spiritualism, we say that the "outside" of the subject is the "thing," i.e., the reality of the body and the world. They are called the "outside" of the subject because there is an invincible non-identity of subject and "thing." Without the body and the world, however, the subject is not what he is, a human subject; the subject needs what he himself is *not*—the body and the world—in order to be a subject. The human subject is not an Absolute Subject but a subject in the world.[1]

[1] In Heidegger's terms, the being of man is *Da-sein* ("there-being"), and the particle *Da* (there) indicates the "ec-centric" character of human subjectivity.

It is not enough, however, to say that being-man is a being-in-the-world. The materialist could use the same expression; man is a small fragment within the cosmos. For us the "being-in" characteristic of man is the "being-in" of a *subject;* the being of man is a being-conscious-in-the-world. Thus man's "being-in" needs to be explicitated as "dwelling," "being familiar with," or "being present to," for such expressions clearly imply a subject.

Note that it would be wrong to think that man is a being dwelling in the world because there *happens* to be a world, as if man could be a conscious being without the world. The term "existence" is meant to express precisely that the human subject is not what he is without the world: if the world is "thought away," the subject can no longer be affirmed. In this sense the world belongs to the essence of man.

The Impossibility of a "Proof"

The statement that man is *existence*[2] cannot be demonstrated in the strict sense of the term. It cannot be demonstrated by the positive sciences of man because man does not occur in them as a subject. These sciences presuppose, but do not prove, a philosophical understanding of man's essence; they are based on the conviction that man's essence is such that it is possible to say something about man by means of scientific models. Secondly, one cannot demonstrate that man's essence is *existence* by deriving it from any prior and more fundamental insight. For nothing is prior and more fundamental for man than his own essence.

The impossibility of a *demonstration*, however, does

[2] From now on we will use italics when the term "existence" is used in its technical sense.

not mean that the philosopher is powerless with respect to his claim or can say about man whatever he fancies. That man is *existence* cannot be demonstrated, but it can be "pointed out": the philosopher can try to let others "see" man's essence as *existence*, just as the materialists and the spiritualists attempted to let us see what man is.

First let us emphasize that the question here regards man on the proper level of his being-man. New-born children, sleeping people, idiots and schizophrenics obviously are not on the proper level of being-human. Such people can still be called human, of course, because in principle they can reach the level of being-human in the proper sense, which cannot be affirmed of a rock or a skunk.

There are several ways in which one can "point out" that man is *existence*. Some authors try to do it through an analysis of consciousness; others prefer to analyze man's bodily being. We will use here the second approach because the first will be discussed in Chapter Two.

Analysis of Man's Bodily Being

One who wishes to speak of the human body must make certain that he does indeed speak of the *human* body. Otherwise he could easily speak of the human body as just another example of the class of bodies and say with the physicist: "The apparent loss of weight of the human body immersed in water is exactly equal to that of the displaced water." Such a statement disregards the *human* aspect of the human body. The human body is *human* because it is "mine," "yours," "hers," in other words, because it is the body of a subject, because it participates in the subject. My grasping hands are "I who grasp," my feet are "I who walk," and my ears are "I who hear." My ears do not belong to the audible world and my feet do not

35

belong to the world that can be walked upon. The *human* body lies on the side of the subject. Considered in this way, man, we must say, *is* his body.

In books about biology, physiology and anatomy, then, the *human* body does not occur because "I," "you," "he" and "she" do not occur in those books. This does not mean that those books do not speak about anything, but it does imply that they do not express the *human* character of the human body.

Once this point is understood, it is easy to see that "my" body is the transition from "me" to my world, that it grafts me on the realm of things and secures for me a solid or shaky standpoint in the world. My hand with five fingers helps me grasp the world in a certain way, different than if I had only one finger on each hand; my feet help me walk on the world in a certain way, different than if I had webfeet or wings; my body helps me occupy a standpoint from which Mount McKinley is high and the sidewalk low, fire is hot and ice is cold. Anything in the world that is soft, hard, red, spatial, light, heavy, fragrant, small, large, etc. points to the human body. A bicycle points to a posture and movements of the body— as do a football, a bed, a house, and all cultural objects.

My body, therefore, lies on the side of the subject who I am but, at the same time, involves me in the world of things; it opens the world to me and signifies my standpoint in it. When my body disintegrates, my world also "goes to pieces," and the complete dissolution of my body means a break with the world, the end also of my being as a conscious-being-in-the-world, the end of my being-man.

Accordingly, reflecting upon the human body, we encounter the subject, who is immersed in the body and, through it, involved in the world. We find the world clinging to the body as a "complex of meanings," we find the body, as human, pointing to the subject. In other words, we find *existence*.

Pact Between Body and the World

The human body itself is a kind of mysterious "knowing" of the world. The body is human because it is the body of a subject, it participates in the subject. The subject, we saw, is a *cogito*, a thinking or knowing subject. Now, if the body participates in the subject, then the body itself also must be called a kind of knowingly being-in-the-world. This actually is the case. If, e.g., I wish to develop a science of colors, I must presuppose that my eyes "know" and can "distinguish" the colors. My body "knows" much better than I do what is meant by hard, soft, sticky, cold, warm, and tasty. The arms and legs, or rather the whole body, of a famous football player "knows" much more about the field, the ball, the goal, the team, space and time than does the player himself. As long as he can rely on this mysterious "knowledge," he is an excellent player, but as soon as he must begin to "reflect," the time has come for him to look for a job as a trainer. My feet "know" much better than I myself the stairs which I climb every day. Similarly, as sexually differentiated, the human body means a bodily "knowing" and "willing" of the other sex, and every personal sexual initiative is based on this mysterious bodily "knowing" and "willing."

A pre-personal subject is at work "underneath" the personal subject; this pre-personal subject is presupposed by every personal knowing and its "prehistory" is taken up in all personal knowing. This pre-personal—one would almost say "anonymous"—subject is the human body. The human body has already concluded a "pact" with the world before the personal subject accomplishes his personal history, and this "pact" is not made superfluous by this personal history. It is, however, a pact concluded in semidarkness, a pact, moreover, which becomes wholly unintelligible when it is replaced by the purely corporeal processes spoken of by the positive sciences. This point is the profound truth contained in psychoanalysis, although Freud himself may not clearly have noted this truth.

The Idea of Essence in Phenomenology

The competent use of the term *existence* presupposes familiarity with all this. Unfortunately, however, this competence is often lacking, and the technical language of phenomenology is then misused to give a semblance of truth to nonsense. This leads some people to conclude that as a "phenomenologist" or an "existentialist" one can say almost anything as long as it is "personal." Many traditional terms, moreover, have a new meaning in phenomenology, which induces people who do not realize this to reject phenomenological thinking.

They complain, for example, that the emphasis placed on *existence* implies a disregard for the classical idea of essence, which is indispensable in any attempt to philosophize. The answer to this complaint is very simple. The accent on *existence* re-emphasizes the idea of essence; when the existential philosopher calls man *existence*, he wishes to say that conscious-being-in-the-world is the essence of man, is that by which man is man and not a thing, a pure spirit, or God. Things, pure spirits and God do not *exist*, that is, they are essentially distinct from man. Because man is essentially conscious-being-in-the-world, man does not enter the world because there happens to be a world. He cannot withdraw from the world and remain man. (One can, of course, withdraw from this or that kind of world to enter a different kind of world.) A complete withdrawal from the world is possible only by death—the end of man as man. *Existence*, then, is an essential characteristic of man, a so-called *existentiale*. He is embodied-subjectivity-in-the-world. This thesis is accepted by very many thinkers today. One of the most important consequences of *existence*, however, is only seen by a few. This consequence is concerned with the ontological status of the world, the mode-of-being of the world and worldly things. Let us consider this point now.

5. The Meaning of the World

If one takes seriously the idea that *existence* expresses an essential aspect of man, there can be no misunderstanding about the ontological status of the world. If man is fastened to the world, then the world is also fastened to man, so that it is impossible to speak about a world-without-man. In other words, the world is radically human.

First Step

This sounds strange and demands explanation. Let us begin with a few simple examples, which are, admittedly, insufficient to fully disclose the human character of the world. I enter the vestibule of a stately mansion and see there lying on the floor a toy pistol and a torn cap in which two long feathers are stuck. These objects are pieces of the world, a little boy's world, and I will not understand anything of them if I do not include the boy in my understanding. Without the presence of the little man to whom they refer, this piece of the world remains meaningless to me. In a similar way, a full ashtray, a well-groomed garden, a bombed-out city cannot be understood without the presence of man.

Thus, we should speak of a world-for-the-farmer, a world-for-the-salesman, a world-for-the-journalist, a world-for-the-politician, etc. All these worlds are essentially world-for-man; without man, that is, without a particular way of being-man, nothing of any of those worlds can be understood: we cannot say what those worlds *are* unless man himself is also named.

One could remark that all those examples merely describe *cultural* worlds, which obviously cannot be understood without man, the creator of culture. But where would the human dimension be in things which I merely "perceive," such as trees, animals, seas and mountains— in a word, the "natural" world? This is the point at which difficulties arise because we have become accustomed to think man and world as divorced from each other. Thus we must ask ourselves whether this "natural" world is also radically human or exists independently of man.

Second Step

The entire world in which the *existent* subject is involved is a *real* world. This statement would be trivial if there were no spiritualistic monism which lets the *reality* of the world evaporate into mere contents of consciousness.

The real world, however, in which man as subject *exists*, is not a world-without-man, not a brute reality, a world "in itself." The thought construct "world-without-man" is a contradiction if man's essence is *existence*. If man as *existence* is fastened to the world, then the world also is fastened to man. I can never ask whether there is a world-without-man or what kind of a world such a world would be: a world-without-man presupposes that man withdraws from the world, a withdrawal which would include also the very question about the world which he is asking. A world-without-man is simply unthinkable, for to conceive such a world would have to imply the possibility of thinking a world without the thinking presence of the *existent* subject.

A world-without-man would be a world of which man is not conscious in any way, a world which he does not affirm in any way. Such a world is simply nothing-for-man: he cannot be conscious of a world of which he is not conscious, or affirm a world which he does not affirm. The thought construct "world-without-man" is a contradiction, a meaningless combination of words, such as square circle. Obviously, no real speaking, no expression of *reality* can be involved here.

The being of the world, however, must be interpreted neither subjectivistically nor objectivistically. A subjectivistic world would be handed over to the subject's arbitrary affirmations, it would cease to be objective *reality*. And an objectivistic world would destroy the subject as *existent* "affirmation" of the world; the subject would no longer be a *real* subject. Worldly reality is not brute reality, but "appearing being," meaning for the subject. Thus the world is a system of meanings. All "being," then, is *per se* meaning, being-for-a-subject, and meaning arises with man.

One could object: granted that it is impossible to *affirm* a world-without-man; nevertheless, there *is* such a world. Such a statement, however, has no meaning, it does not express any reality. By using the term "is," man affirms the being of something. But man cannot affirm that something *is* if he thinks himself away as an *existent* subject; in other words, he never affirms anything other than

41

being-for-man. "To be" has no other meaning than "to be for man." Without man, therefore, there is no world-for-man. What *else* could I say?

Laplace's Primitive Nebula as a World-Without-Man

According to Laplace, our earth was formed from a primitive nebula, whose physical conditions were such that for a long time no life, and certainly no human life, was possible. That nebula existed before man and, consequently, without man. What sense does it make, then, to assert that without man there is no world?

Any phenomenologist knows that the earth is much older than the "first man" and that scientists speak of a world dating from before man. But, does this mean that the geologists speak of a world-without-geologists? *This and nothing else is the issue.* What remains of Laplace's primitive nebula, of his calculations and formulae if we think away the presence in the world of Laplace's subjectivity or the subjectivity of those who take over his intentions? Nothing whatsoever.

The same conclusion continues to impose itself: the world is radically human, and the truth about this world is radically human. Without man's subjectivity no affirmation of reality has any meaning, and without the affirmation of *reality* all assertions are an idle playing with words. The world is not the sum total of brute realities, which are what they are-without-man, in themselves, in an "absolutely objective" and isolated way. Some of the sharpest minds among scientists realize this when they say that the physical sciences do not speak of "nature in itself" (Heisenberg). Sometimes, however, they use unfortunate expressions; for instance, when they say that the physical sciences do not express "objectivity." But what they intend to say is evident enough: "objectivity" refers to an *objectivistic* world, a world in itself, divorced from the subject.

The "in Itself" According to Sartre

Sartre's vain attempt to speak of brute reality also illustrates that it is impossible to do so. Sartre radically opposes two types of being: the "in itself" or the material thing and the "for itself" or consciousness. Only the material thing is fully being; it is perfect positivity, it is what it is, fully self-identical; it maintains no relations, includes no negation, does not posit itself as different from anything else; it is not created and has no ground of being, it simply *is*.

These enigmatic expressions become somewhat clearer if we keep in mind that "relations," "being different," "ground of being," and similar terms presuppose consciousness. Since the "in itself" has no consciousness, it follows, Sartre thinks, that it maintains no relations, has no ground of being, etc.

The "for itself" or consciousness, on the other hand, always needs the "in itself" to be consciousness. For consciousness is always consciousness of something other than consciousness itself. Consciousness is essentially orientated to the "in itself," it is intentional. Consciousness, moreover, Sartre adds, is essentially negative, it "nihilates." If, for example, I am conscious of this ashtray, this means that I am *not* (*nihil*) this ashtray, not identical with this ashtray. Consciousness, then, is always pure "nihilation." Even if I am conscious of myself as a waiter or as just, this simply means that I am conscious of not being identical with the waiter or the just man, for tomorrow I may cease being a waiter or just. Even in my self-consciousness, then, I "nihilate" my own identity.

Thus consciousness always says *distance*, not being

43

that of which one is conscious. Consciousness breaks the fullness of being found in the "in itself," it is negativity, a "disease of being," nothingness.

Critique. Sartre is right, of course, when he says that all consciousness is consciousness of something and always contains a negative aspect. When I am conscious of something, I am indeed conscious of a certain *distance* with respect to this something; I am not identical with this ashtray; I am not identical with the waiter or the just man who I am. But when Sartre claims that consciousness is *nothing but* nihilation, he simply disregards all positive aspects of consciousness. The first phenomenological evidence, however, is precisely the *affirmation* of that of which I am conscious: I affirm the ashtray, the waiter or the just man, I affirm the reality of all this. Is this affirmation a negation? Obviously not.

Secondly, Sartre describes the "in itself" as full positivity. He conceives this "in itself" as brute reality, but fails to take into consideration that the only being of which he can speak is always "appearing being," being as presenting itself to consciousness. His description of the "in itself" as maintaining no relations, having no ground, etc. assumes that it is possible to know something while "thinking away" the encounter in which this something presents itself to the knower. He simply takes what the "in itself" is "for us," drops the "for us," and imagines that he can describe the "in itself" by assigning to it the opposite of all the qualifications that must be asserted of the "in itself for us." Sartre forgets that no one can talk about being "in itself" independently of his consciousness. His attempt to speak of the "in itself" as divorced from consciousness fails because it is impossible to speak about a world from which the conscious subject is "thought away." Sartre relapses here into the Cartesian split between subject and world.

Not One World-in-Itself, but Many Human Worlds

If the world and the truth about the world are radically human, it follows that there are many human worlds, corresponding to the many attitudes or standpoints of the *existent* subject. The meaning of the word differs according as the subject-in-the-world occupies a different standpoint.

As we saw, Descartes claimed that in brute reality only that is objective reality which can be expressed in quantitative terms. This amounted to asserting that only one world—the world-for-the-physicist—can be called objective. Through the influence of Descartes and Locke, this conviction became firmly embedded in Western thought; the world, the world-in-itself, is the world-for-the-physicist. Even the world-for-the-physicist, however, is a human world, connected with the physicist's intentional relationship with the world. The world-for-the-physicist is just one of the many possible worlds, his standpoint is just one among many others.

What, for example is water for me? It is something I use for washing and drinking. But if I love bathing, water reveals itself under an entirely different aspect: I like to plunge into the "cooling waves." Water is also an extinguisher, but I could not know this meaning if I did not know what fire is and what is meant by putting out a fire. For a fisherman water is not an extinguisher or a cooling wave: he faces water with an entirely different attitude, so that water has an entirely different meaning for him. No one ever goes fishing in an extinguisher. A skater who slides underneath the ice sees a most terrifying aspect of water, but no one ever froze to death in the cooling waves. Finally, to finish with another arbitrary example, there is one standpoint from which water is H_2O—the standpoint

45

of the chemist. Outside this standpoint, this attitude of chemical "interest," water is not H_2O. No boy ever takes his girl out to SiO_4 covered with H_2O and an admixture of NaCl: they go, instead, to the beach.

Again, what is the meaning of human nakedness? This depends entirely on the many possible standpoints of the subject: it may be artistic, medical, sexual, athletic, hygienic, etc.

A general theory of man's standpoints or attitudes cannot easily be formulated. We will limit ourselves here to the following provisional remarks. A first group of attitudes is man's bodily being. The fact that man is a being with arms and legs, hands and feet, eyes, ears and a nose, means that he is involved in many different worlds in many different ways. We say "different" worlds, for in man's visual world there are no sounds, in his audible world there is nothing to see, and in his graspable world nothing is tasty.

A second group of attitudes is connected with man's "realms of affairs." It makes sense to speak of a world for the farmer, the professor, the revolutionary, the hunter, the salesman, etc. These worlds differ from one another, and the things in these worlds refer to one another in different ways. For the hunter the gun refers to other things than it does for the revolutionary; for a scholar the book forms part of a different system of meanings than it has for a publisher or a dealer in used paper. In every case, however, the particular system of meanings becomes intelligible by way of one's understanding of a particular "realm of affairs."

Thirdly, love could be mentioned as a standpoint. But, until we have analyzed love, we cannot say much about this standpoint. If, however, one is willing to include in the "world" the economic, social and political structures of society, it should be obvious that this "world" offers different aspects according as man is or is not animated by the desire and the will to foster an increasing recognition of man by man. One who lives and breathes humanity lives in another world than one who thinks that other people are there only to cringe as slaves at his feet.

Fourthly, the various phases of history need to be mentioned as standpoints which codetermine the facet presented by the world. Only in a particular phase of history does it become possible to see a particular facet of the world. One who does not yet stand in that phase simply does not see that aspect of the world. For example, one who still lives in the era of sheer individualism does not see the demands imposed upon him by the intrinsically social character of man.

We are now far removed from the view that "here" is the subject, divorced from the world, and "there" a world-in-itself, which is mirrored in the subject's consciousness. Yet this view has become almost "second nature" in Western thought: it is simply taken for granted that it is so. A "reversal" (Heidegger) is needed to make man abandon a standpoint which has become his "natural attitude" (Husserl).

Is Our View a Kind of Psychologism?

The objection could be raised that we are indulging in a kind of psychologism; we take meanings which lie "in" consciousness, project them "outside" on things, and then ascribe these meanings to the things themselves. The special meanings of water for the fisherman, the swimmer or the drinker, the objection argues, lie only in consciousness and should not be attributed to water itself.

This objection is based on two untenable assumptions. The first is that consciousness is locked up in itself and contains meanings which we project upon "things." The

47

second is that the "things themselves" are brute realities, of which, for example, the chemist is entitled to tell us what they are. But consciousness is not locked up in itself and is not a locker containing meanings belonging to it in itself. Being-conscious is a mode of being-in-the-world. Secondly, there is no such thing as brute reality, but there are *existent* subjects and human worlds corresponding to these subjects. Finally, if the "cooling waves" must be called a psychological meaning because it cannot be defined independently of the subject, the same must be said of H_2O. This meaning clings to the attitude which makes man a chemist, and without that specific attitude the formula H_2O does not say anything. The "reciprocal implication of subject and world" (Kwant) is the original dimension in which man stands, thinks and speaks. If he places himself outside this dimension, he no longer stands anywhere and does not speak of anything.

6. The "Primitive Fact" of Existential Phenomenology

The expression "reciprocal implication of subject and world" indicates what some thinkers call the "primitive fact" or the "central reference point" (Marcel) of existential phenomenology. Let us clarify these terms.

In every great philosophy there is an original intuition, an all-encompassing "light" which makes it possible for the thinker to bring clarity to the complexity of reality. Such an intuition can be found in Aristotle, Descartes, Kant, Hegel, Marx, etc. No philosophy is satisfied with a disorderly enumeration of things: philosophy is not "a tale told by an idiot." The philosopher tries to find unity in plurality, he wishes to "com-prehend" (Brunschwicg). But he does not know how this is to be done *a priori*. A new philosophy begins with the vague expectation that a certain approach will be fruitful, but the philosopher does not yet realize exactly what he is doing or which "light" guides him in his work. Generally speaking, the evident sterility of a certain approach used in the past induces him to try a different approach. What this different way of thinking is, however, remains provisionally obscure.

It can happen, for example, that a psychologist finds a physiological explanation of puberty insufficient and therefore tries a new approach. His primary intention is to explain puberty, and not to reflect upon his new approach itself. Only later does this approach itself become a topic of reflection, and often the man who reflects upon it is not the one who was first to make use of it. Thus it could happen that the philosophies of Husserl and Heidegger were much better understood by others than by these two thinkers themselves.

A philosophy will be fruitful to the extent that its "primitive fact" can throw light on the complexity of reality and establish unity in it. Using the ideas "large elephant" or "hard rock" is entirely fruitless for they explain nothing, but the concept "matter" leads at least to some results.

One can easily understand now that at one time there were existentialists and phenomenologists, but practically no one could define either existentialism or phenomenology. These terms seemed to have as many meanings as there were existentialists and phenomenologists. This need not surprise us. Philosophizing is a way of living and shares in the lack of transparency which characterizes life itself. Moreover, it exists as a "style" of thinking before it becomes a topic of explicit attention.

At present, these difficulties have been overcome. It is now generally agreed that the idea of *existence* or intentionality is the "primitive fact," the central intuition, the all-pervading "moment" of intelligibility of the new style.

49

Suitable Terms

A search has been made for others terms expressing as unambiguously as possible the central reference point of existential phenomenology, the impossibility of divorcing subject and world. *Encounter* is perhaps one of the best. For an encounter requires two terms: a subject who encounters, and something encountered by the subject. If either is missing, there is no encounter.

Dialogue also is suitable, for it implies that two "partners" contribute their share. If one partner is "thought away," there is no dialogue. The unity of subject and world is the unity of a dialogue, a dialectical unity.

There are still other terms. Marcel prefers *participation*, in the double sense of having part and taking part in the world. Merleau-Ponty speaks of *presence*. This term also is very clear: presence is not conceivable unless there is a subject of presence and something which is present to the subject.

Is Man Nothing but Being-Conscious-in-the-World?

These reflections, however, do not yet sufficiently clarify the "primitive fact" of existential phenomenology. Undoubtedly it is true that all philosophizing is always and of necessity concerned with man as *existence*, as reciprocal implication of subject and world. But one would go too far by claiming that man's being is *exclusively* a being-conscious-*in*-the-world, that is, that in man there is *nothing but* the relationship of subjectivity and world. If that were true, love and hatred could no longer be what they are. While love and hatred are also related to the world, one cannot say that they are nothing but modes of the subject's relationship to a worldly object. Justified as the philosopher is in his critical attitude, he has no right *a priori* to exclude certain possible forms of reality. The primitive fact of a philosophy escapes the charge of dogmatism only if it is accepted in faithfulness to reality.

There are forms of existential-phenomenological thinking in which *existence* is *exclusively* understood as the unity of reciprocal implication of subject and *world*. This certainly is the case with the atheistic existentialism of Sartre and Merleau-Ponty. When Merleau-Ponty says that man as subject is *nothing but* a project of his world, he arbitrarily encapsulates man in one dimension of *existence*, restricting him to openness to worldly reality. Such an *a priori* position at once gives a philosophy an atheistic character. When it is taken, the "affirmation" of God can only be the affirmation of a deified worldly reality or of a degraded Transcendent Reality reduced to a worldly status; it can never be what it is supposed to be, viz., the "affirmation" of the Transcendent as Transcendent.

Accordingly, we must be more prudent and abstain from excluding a possible realm of reality *a priori*. For us, then, the primitive fact of existential phenomenology is *existence* or intentionality, conceived as the openness of the subject to *everything* which is not the subject himself. This "everything" certainly includes the world. Terms such as "encounter," "dialogue," "participation" and "presence" can be retained; they are sufficiently flexible to be used in an enlarged sense if subsequently there would be any need for it.

Suggested Readings

William A. Luijpen, *Existential Phenomenology*, revised ed., Pittsburgh, 1969, Ch. 1.

Albert Dondeyne, *Contemporary European Thought and Christian Faith*, 3rd impr., Pittsburgh, 1968.

51

Karl Jaspers, *Ways to Wisdom*, New Haven, 1954.

Maurice Merleau-Ponty, *Sense and Nonsense*, Evanston, Ill., 1964.

René Descartes, *Discourse on Method*.

CHAPTER TWO

Phenomenology of Knowledge

IN THE PRECEDING PAGES we made use of an insight for which no justification was yet presented: we spoke of human knowledge as if we knew what knowledge is. But when I wonder what knowledge is, I have to admit that I cannot at once answer this question. Strange as it seems, however, the fact that I did not "really" know what knowledge is did not cause any special difficulties.

Wondering why, I find that the answer is not too difficult: I cannot honestly admit that I do not "really" know what it is to know. I can distinguish knowing a person and loving him, and this implies that I know what knowledge is and what love is. As soon, however, as I try to *express* what knowledge is, my tongue is tied. The same happened to Augustine when he wondered what time is.

1. EXPLICITATION

This "really" knowing while being unable to express it is my presence to the knowing being I am. When a psychologist tries to know a fellowman, this man is the topic of his knowledge. He will say, for example, that this man is an introvert, emotional and intelligent. In thus expressing the terminus of his knowing encounter, the psychologist "omits" his own knowing and all the steps leading to his judgment: he does not express them. Nevertheless, he knows what psychological knowledge is and how he forms his judgment. Because he is present to the knower he himself is, he can make this knowing itself the theme of his consideration.

The same happens all the time in other situations. Counting the cigarettes in my pack, I express the terminus encountered by my act of counting by saying: "There are twelve." My counting itself, however, is omitted, it does not become the theme of my consideration. Nevertheless, I know what counting is because I am present to my act of counting. As soon as anyone asks me what I am doing, I answer: "I am counting." At that very moment, the theme of my knowing is no longer the cigarettes but my counting itself. In counting, I *am* present to my counting, but when I am asked what I am doing, I *place* myself explicitly in the presence of my counting and give expression to it.

Pre-reflective Consciousness and the "Unreflected"

Accordingly, there is an implicit, non-thematic, non-reflective consciousness, which consists of a simple presence to what I am doing. This consciousness is called "counting-consciousness," "love-consciousness," "perception-consciousness," etc. It is not a consciousness *of* counting, *of* love, *of* perception. Originally there is no consciousness *of* self, but self-consciousness compenetrates consciousness *of* something. By my consciousness I *am* originally present to myself; by reflection I *place* myself in my presence, so that that which at first I "omitted"—my love, acting, or knowing—becomes the theme of my consciousness.

Pre-reflective consciousness is extremely important. Philosophizing begins in it, for in the first instance philosophizing is nothing but the expression of life itself. Life

—being knowingly, actively, lovingly, desiringly, emotionally in the world—is a being-conscious-in-the-world, a non-thematic consciousness. Reflective consciousness, however, is continually fed by this unreflective dimension of life, which it thematizes. If it does not thematize unreflective life, our philosophizing "hangs in the air" without any support. Philosophy, then, may never contradict the unreflective dimension, but must try to seize "life" and give expression to it.

To return now to the question what knowledge is, an answer is possible because I am present to the knower who I myself am. The answer will have to consist in the explicitation of my knowledge-consciousness, so that the latter becomes consciousness *of* knowledge. The answer does not "demonstrate," but merely "points out" and expresses that to which I am present.

The history of thought shows how easily the philosopher can disregard an essential aspect of unreflected life. It can happen that an entire generation of thinkers remains totally blind to a particular phenomenon because of all kinds of prejudices and unquestioned convictions. If a discovery is too far ahead of its time, the ingenious thinker who does "see" has no other choice than to work first at the "education" which can prepare his contemporaries for seeing what he sees. Let us add that certain insights require a long preparation before they can be born in history. This point is illustrated by the history of man's definition of knowledge.

2. REALISM AND IDEALISM

Since Descartes philosophers accepted without question that knowledge was a mirroring of brute reality and that physical science was *the* system of objective mirror im-

55

ages. We must now add that the same view also resulted
from Locke's philosophy although this thinker began with
a radically different starting point.

Primary and Secondary Qualities

Locke rejected innate ideas and held that man's cognitive power is like a piece of paper on which nothing is
written; the "writing" has to be done from without and by
experience alone. Locke distinguished "ideas in the mind"
and "qualities in the body." The former are produced by
the latter. Next, he distinguished primary and secondary
qualities. The primary qualities of things, such as shape,
are open to more than one sense organ; secondary qualities are the proper object of one sense organ only; for
instance color and odor. According to Locke, the ideas of
the primary qualities are objective, while those of secondary qualities are subjective. For warm water can produce
in one hand a feeling of heat and, at the same time, in the
other hand a feeling of cold, but a shape can never produce the idea of a square through one hand and that of a
sphere through the other.

This apparently rather innocent distinction contains an
implicit theory of knowledge. For as long as knowledge is
conceived as the knowing subject's immediate presence to
a present reality, one cannot possibly claim that only the
primary qualities are objective. In the subject's immediate
presence to an apple, shape as well as odor are given as
present realities, as objective. Thus Locke's distinction
implied that knowledge is not the subject's immediate
presence to a present reality, and it left him no alternative
but to consider knowledge as a purely passive mirroring
of a world divorced from the subject. If the knowing
subject is understood as a passive and worldless subject
and the world is conceived as a collection of things-in-

themselves divorced from the subject, then one can say that only the primary qualities are objective. This statement then means that only the quantitative aspects are accurately mirrored. With respect to secondary qualities accurate mirroring was held to be impossible because the knower was thought to spoil the mirroring through his subjective contributions to the knowing act.

Despite differences, then, Descartes and Locke are fundamentally in agreement about the definition of knowledge: knowledge is a mirroring in a worldless subject of a world divorced from the subject, and *the* system of objective mirroring is that of physical science because only this science operates with the categories of quantity. For both Descartes and Locke *ideas* are the direct objects of man's knowledge. This meant that the so-called "critical problem" was concerned with the reality in the "outside" world of those things whose ideas were present "inside" consciousness.

A Twofold Possibility

Given the divorce between subject and world, more emphasis could be placed on either consciousness or the world. Thus we can distinguish idealism and realism. Idealism puts the main emphasis on consciousness, its priority, spontaneity and activity. For Descartes, consciousness was still coupled to the world although his methodic doubt had, strictly speaking, made any connection impossible. Idealism tried to overcome this connection and eliminate the world entirely as a source of knowledge. In the eyes of the idealist, the perception of the world, with its implied darkness and confusion, is an inauthentic form of knowledge that should be replaced by the clarity of the self-sufficient idea, pure self-reflection.

Realism went to the opposite extreme. Realism is born

57

from the fundamental insight that our consciousness is "sensitive" and passive. It is undeniably true that the reality of things *imposes* itself on our perceiving consciousness, that perception *finds* reality. For this reason the realists have always rejected innate ideas and maintained that all knowledge arises from the experience of reality. "Reality," however, for the realist, is the brute reality of an inhuman world, divorced from the subject. "Thinking away" man's perceiving consciousness from the world, the realist thought that he could speak of a world-without-man and that man's consciousness faces this world as pure passivity, as a *tabula rasa*, a piece of paper on which nothing is written, a mirror in which a fully isolated world inscribes or impresses itself. Thus, the world is purely a spectacle for consciousness; as a "detached spectator," the knower considers the world without having a standpoint in it.

Realism, however, did not manage to build a bridge between consciousness and world. For in realism consciousness occurs only as divorced from the world, although knowledge is said to be objective, that is, in agreement with a reality which is isolated from the knower. There is in the knower a mirror image, an "impressed species": reality impresses in the knowing subject an image, which, as a replica of reality-in-itself, is the proper object of knowledge. Accordingly, I never know a chair, a house or a plant, but only a chair-impression, a house-impression, a plant-impression. Having dogmatically accepted an encapsulated consciousness and a world-in-itself, realism failed to build a bridge between consciousness and the world.

A "Scientific Theory of Perception

To explain the existence of perception-impressions, psychologists let themselves be guided by their admiration for physical science; they proceeded to study all contents of consciousness with the same method with which the physicist studies matter, viz., the analysis of matter into its ultimate constituent elements. In this way a house-impression was to be reduced to its component elements. These elements, it was thought, could be found in the elementary sensations, caused by physical stimuli, exercising a unilateral and physically determining influence upon human sensitivity. A house-impression could ultimately be constructed by means of the summation of innumerable elementary sensations caused by those stimuli, and this summation was assumed to come about through the mechanism of association.

Other psychologists, however, considered such a way of speaking about perception not sufficiently "scientific." They argued that "scientific" speech should not mention perception but speak of nerve paths, cerebral processes, etc. Psychology had to be a kind of physiology, perception could be objective only insofar as a physical science could express it.

A Blooming Tree in a Meadow

What does all this mean? It would appear most trivial that when I speak of a blooming tree in a meadow, I wish to claim to speak of a blooming tree in a meadow. The physical sciences can say something about that tree and my perception of it. They register all kinds of physical and physiological processes, they can make the cerebral processes perceptible by means of instruments and present their course in curves. But what sense does it make to wish to speak *only in this way* about the perception of a blooming tree in the meadow? Must a blooming tree be reduced to a vacuum in which here and there scattered electric charges move about with great velocity? It does not make sense to say that we "naturally" perceive a blooming tree and then to replace the tree by the "ingredients" of various sciences, in order to let these sciences determine what is really objective, in a blooming tree. They have no competency in this question. When there is question of perceiving a tree, should we not leave the tree where it is? The tree is not a series of processes in our brain but a tree-in-the-meadow.

What the sciences say about cerebral processes in perception is true, but, we must ask, how do the scientists know what they are speaking about? When they speak of cerebral processes and electrical charges in connection with my perception, *they do not speak of anything at all* unless ultimately they are trying to speak of the perception of the blooming tree in the meadow. But in that case it does not make sense to *replace* the tree by a system of meanings disclosed by those sciences and to *substitute* ingredients of those sciences for perception itself.

Husserl's call, then, "Back to the things themselves," was an invitation to philosophy to return to the original experience of the original world. The world-for-the-physicist is not this original world but built upon the original world, and the experience of physical science is not the original experience but built upon original experience. Knowledge must be explicitated in terms of the integral way in which it occurs.

3. HUMAN KNOWLEDGE AS INTENTIONALITY

Phenomenology calls the subject-as-*cogito*, the knowing subject, "intentionality." Scholastic philosophy used the same term when it assigned to the substitute cognitive images—"impressed species"—the role of building a bridge between the encapsulated subject and brute reality. Those images, it was said, have only "intentional being": their whole being consists in their referring to reality.

When Husserl uses the term "intentionality," however, he does not refer to an encapsulated subject and a world-in-itself, but he describes the knowing subject as orientation-to or openness-to-the world. Knowledge is not a matter of "strong cognitive images" in the subject's interiority, but the *immediate* presence of the subject as a kind of "light" to a present reality. Knowledge is a mode of man's being-involved-in-the-world. The subject, then, is not "first" and in himself a kind of "psychical thing" which "subsequently" enters into relationship with physical things through cognitive images. Knowledge is not a relationship between two different realities, but is the subject himself involved in the world.

Is the "Critical Problem" Talked Out of Existence Here?

In Chapter One we mentioned that the critical problem, as it has been formulated since Descartes, is a pseudo-problem. Human knowledge really occurs only as intentionality, and this means that knowledge simply is not what it is without the real world. The reality of the world cannot and need not be proved, for the knowing subject himself is relation-to-the-real world. The "scandal of philosophy" is not that no one has ever managed to offer a valid proof for the reality of the world (Kant), but the fact that people continue to look for such a proof (Heidegger).

But, one will argue with Descartes, can I not dream and, while dreaming, think that I perceive a real world even though I do not really perceive such a world? Obviously, I can do so. But the fact that Descartes himself distinguished between perceiving and dreaming shows that he implicitly recognized the difference between a perceived world and a dreamt world: he recognized that, while perceiving, he was involved in a real world and that he was not so involved when he dreamt. Nevertheless, by including the world of perception in his doubt, Descartes wiped out the distinction between perceiving and dreaming, for this distinction exists by virtue of the difference between a perceived world and a dreamt world. In the images with which Descartes filled consciousness, the knowing subject can never "see" whether they are dream images or images of reality.

One who takes the idea of intentionality seriously no longer asks whether the world which he "sees" is real, but he can ask himself whether he really "sees" or merely dreams.

Phenomenological Realism

Phenomenology's idea of intentionality excludes idealism. The knowing subject is intentional, he is orientation to that which is not the subject himself. Thus the knowing subject is never purely active but always *also* receptive, "sensitive" to a reality which is not the subject himself. The knower is not the creator but merely the "shepherd" of reality (Heidegger).

Realism also, in its traditional form, is made impossible by the idea of intentionality. The world, as conceived by phenomenology, is the *real* world. The correlate of the *existent* subject-as-*cogito* is the "unconcealed," that which shows itself, which discloses itself, appearing being itself. Phenomenology calls appearing being "meaning." Meaning is the real which imposes itself on the knowing subject. But the fact that the real *imposes* itself does not give anyone the right to conceive the real as an "in itself," for the "in itself" would be something which in principle is cut off from the subject and therefore cannot even impose itself on the subject.

Accordingly, the traditional dilemma, "either idealism or realism," is not a genuine dilemma. Phenomenology itself may be called a realistic philosophy, but the term "realistic" should not be understood in the objectivistic sense in which it is taken by traditional or representational realism. To distinguish "reality" as it is understood by phenomenology from the "reality in itself" of representational realism, the terms "in itself for us" or "being for us" are widely used; they express that worldly meaning has *autonomy of being* but always *in reference to* the subject.

The World as System of "Nearby" and "Remote" Meanings

When I see a house, I do not hesitate to say that I really see a house, even though it is true that I merely perceive a particular *profile* of it. I could see the unseen parts of the house if I changed my spatial standpoint, but then I would no longer see the profile I saw first. In principle I can perceive an endless number of profiles because I can occupy innumerable different standpoints with respect to the house.

The different profiles of the perception-object are connected with one another, for every profile of the perceived object intrinsically refers to the other profiles which will appear when I change my standpoint. If there were no intrinsic reference, there would be no real perception: my perception of Peter's face implies the possibility of perceiving his back if Peter is real. A backless Peter would be a mere fancy. Without this internal reference to other possible profiles, that which actually appears is not what it is. It is this continuous internal reference that unites the different profiles, making the object a system of "nearby" and "remote" meanings.

The object of perception shows also an external *horizon*. The totality of the perception-object is also united

63

with the entire *field* of perception. Every object appears as a particular "figure" against an horizon of meanings. The apple which I perceive as a unity and totality in an endless series of profiles, appears as a real apple only against the horizon of the table or fruitbowl on which it lies. An apple which does not lie on a table, hang on a tree, or is in a child's hand—an apple which does not appear against any background—simply is not a real apple, not an object of real perception, but an imaginary apple. The very perception of an apple essentially includes its background or horizon.

Because I direct my attention to the apple and not to the child's hand in which it lies, the apple appears to me as an emphasized figure, a meaning which is, as it were, cut out and brought forward from the background of meanings. But this background—the hand, the arm and the child's body, the floor on which he stands, the room and the house—is co-constitutive for the real apple. An apple which does not have an external horizon cannot be perceived and is not real.

Accordingly, perception is always perception of the whole thing, integrated in a more-encompassing field, and this field itself is taken up into an horizon of more distant meanings. The totality of this complex system of ever-evanescent, "nearby" and "remote" meanings, clinging to the ever-evanescent moments of perception's actuality and potentiality, phenomenology calls the "world."

The Phenomenological "Reduction" and the "Lived World"

Husserl's search for an authentically philosophical conception of experience led him to the idea of intentionality. Some of the implications of this idea were described above and they pointed to the answer to be given to the question about the importance of the "phenomenological reduction." Before describing its function, however, we would like to devote a few words to a particular view of this reduction which is no longer acceptable.

When Husserl defined the knowing subject as intentionality, he "bracketed" the actual existence of the worldly meaning to which the subject is orientated, that is, he suspended judgment about the existence of this meaning, because he did not wish to get caught in the hopeless controversy between idealism and realism. He did not yet see at the time that one can "bracket" the existence of meaning only if one presupposes that there is an isolated consciousness, filled with contents. Gradually, however, Husserl became aware of the fact that his idea of intentionality eliminated that presupposition. This led him eventually to abandon the phenomenological reduction, conceived as the "bracketing" of the existence of meaning. In Heidegger and Merleau-Ponty one does not even find a trace of such "bracketing."

On the other hand Husserl increasingly emphasized the necessity of the phenomenological reduction. He gradually began to see that all scientific statements presuppose and are based upon a more fundamental experience than scientific experience, and that precisely for this reason scientists know what they are speaking about. This much more fundamental experience is the conscious subject himself with his many different attitudes, and the correlate of that experience is the "lived world."

Conceived as the return to our most original experience of our most original world, the phenomenological reduction is an essential part of phenomenological philosophy. When there is question of perceiving a blooming tree in the meadow, I can call all kinds of sciences to my assistance, but I only know what the results of their investigations mean because I know what is meant by the "ordinary" perception of a blooming tree in the meadow. If the sciences do not ultimately speak of a world in which the sun rises and sets, a world in which girls are pretty and boys handsome, a world in which, by simply going on vacation, I can learn what a sea, a river, a mountain is, then even the most intelligent scientist does not know what he is speaking of. The sciences do not know of what they speak unless they accept the fact that ultimately they merely explicitate an experience that is much more original than that of science and a world that is much more original than the world disclosed by the sciences. The primarily real and objective world is the world in which the physicist is happily or unhappily married, in which he is warm or cold, regardless of what the thermometer says, and in which, just before sunset, he bought a book explaining that the sun does not set.

In the lived world there is a great difference between the soft red of a rug, the sticky red of drying blood, the healthy red of a youthful face, and the seductive red of painted lips. When science speaks of "certain movements of the nostrils and contractions of the corners of the mouth, accompanied by twinkling of the eyes," the scientist knows that it speaks of a smile only because he has previously experienced what it means that someone smiled at him.

The "return to the things themselves" is the return to the lived world, and this return implies the recognition of the *existent* subject with his many standpoints as the most original experience of the world. To recognize this subject is to execute the phenomenological reduction. The experience of the lived world used to be—and still is—characterized by the sciences as "merely" subjective and relative. In actual fact, however, this experience is the ultimate foundation, thanks to which the scientists know what they really talk about. Thus the meanings of the lived world cannot be replaced by a system of meanings disclosed by the sciences, and the experience of the sciences cannot be substituted for the much more original experience upon which scientific experience is based. Scientism, which tries to do so, is a philosophy of experience which disregards its own origin.

4. SENSITIVE AND SPIRITUAL KNOWING

The commonplace distinction between sensitive and spiritual knowing is often incorrectly presented. It is simply posited at the very start as, e.g., the difference between sensitive seeing and intellectual understanding, after which the authors proceed to speak of sensitive knowing, *divorced* from intellectual knowing, as if these ways of knowing are not only distinguishable but also separable. Animals and man, so it is said, have seeing in common, but only man understands; hence only this power distinguishes man from the animal.

Such a way of speaking goes against the most immediate evidence. There is no purely sensitive seeing in man, a seeing that is not permeated with spiritual consciousness or understanding. If the term "seeing" is supposed to refer to a purely sensitive activity, man does not have any sight. Man and animal do not have sight in common.

On the other hand, in animals there is something which more or less resembles that which in man is seeing. The animal's behavior cannot be understood without allowing certain "shadows of knowledge" (Buytendijk). But if the animal's seeing is a purely sensitive form of knowing, man does not know what it is like because he has no experience of such acts of knowing.

A Difficult Distinction

Difficult as it is to find the distinction between sensitive and intellectual knowing in reality, it should not be en-

67

tirely rejected. For my knowing of a worldly object shows "moments" which are irreducible to one another. Let us look again at the example of the table.

The particular profile I actually see depends on the particular standpoint I occupy. To perceive a different profile, I must change my standpoint. This means that my perception of this table here is determined by spatial conditions. These conditions are, at the same time, temporal conditions: I see *here and now* something other than I will see *later there* or saw *earlier yonder*. A change in the spatio-temporal conditions of perception also modifies perception itself.

On the other hand, I also understand what a table is and I realize that this understanding does not change when the spatio-temporal conditions are modified. Throughout all changing conditions of space and time, I unchangeably understand what a table is.

Knowledge, then, contains at least "two" moments which are not simply equivalent. My consciousness depends on spatio-temporal conditions but, on the other hand, it does not depend on them. These two "moments," therefore, cannot be wholly identical. Understanding transcends the relativity affecting sense perception, it is not affected by the relationship to spatio-temporal standpoints.

It is very difficult to correctly understand the distinction between sense perception and understanding. One could easily be tempted to isolate the understanding of the object's essence from the sensitive consciousness of its "this, here and now," as if the spirit seized "only" the essence and the "this, here and now" would be purely accidental to this essence. Sense knowledge, on the other hand, would be limited to the concrete and changeable aspects of the object. As a matter of fact, however, human knowledge is undivided: my seeing, hearing, feeling, etc.

are permeated with spiritual consciousness; and my spiritual understanding is never isolated from sense knowledge.

The Concept

The proper character of understanding manifests itself even better if we pay attention to its terminus. Through my understanding, a particular thing is constituted as a certain essence-for-me, an intelligible meaning for me. This essence imposes itself upon me; I cannot arbitrarily give any meaning I fancy to the world. A chair represents a different intelligible meaning than does a cigar or a plant. My understanding, then, is a dialogue between me and the essence of the thing understood.

This dialogue finds a provisional terminus in the expression I give to what I understand. This expression results from my understandingly-being-in-the-world and is known as "idea" or "concept." The result of understanding this tree or this cigar is the concept "tree" or "cigar." Through my understanding, I dwell in my world as a system of intelligible meanings, but insofar as I express that intelligibility in my ideas and embody it in words, I dwell in a "world of ideas."

We come very close here to Plato; there certainly is a "world of ideas." Plato was right when he saw that the knower is not merely open to the mutable shape of things but also "possesses" immutable ideas. But thinking that from the encounter with the mutable world no immutable ideas could ever arise, Plato posited an independent world of ideas, contemplated by the soul in a mysterious pre-existence. In this way he tried to account for the fact that man does possess immutable ideas. Today, Plato's myth is superfluous. There is a world of ideas, but this world is not autonomous: it is produced by me and my world. As a

69

knowing subject I dwell in the world on "two" levels, and on "one" of these levels I dwell in a world of essences. I express this dwelling in immutable ideas, which I embody in language. In this way I dwell in a "world of ideas."

Because the term "spiritual" was very often misunderstood in an exaggerated spiritualistic sense, some contemporary thinkers dislike the term "spiritual understanding"; it seems to disregard the fact that man is whatever he is only on the basis of matter. Obviously, however, we do not use the term as if spiritual meant *purely* spiritual. In a similar way the term "immutable idea" does not mean to deny the historicity of our understanding and our concepts: it merely expresses that understanding does not change when the spatio-temporal conditions of perception change.

The Abstracting and Universalizing Character of Understanding

Our understandingly dwelling in the world implies a special organization of the world. A certain aspect of the object considered—that which is essential to it—is drawn into the foreground of my field of presence, and the concrete and individual features are pushed into the background. Thus my concept "house," "stop light" or "island" does not say anything about the concrete and individual aspects of those objects. This means that my understanding is abstractive and my concept abstract.

Strictly speaking, the terms "abstractive" and "abstract" could even be used in connection with the figure-horizon structure of perception. If I look for the biggest apple in the fruit bowl, the apples come forward as a figure and the other fruit become background. And among the apples, again, only one—the biggest—becomes a pronounced figure. Usually, however, we speak of abstraction only with respect to understanding; I bring the essence forward as a pronounced figure, while the individual characteristics are shifted to the horizon. Because my concept does not express the individual characteristic of the terminus of my knowing encounter, my "world of ideas" contains only one idea "house," "island" or "horse." The abstract idea retains only an implicit reference to the individual; it connotes that the concept can be realized only in the individual. The abstract concept is an "open" concept.

The abstract character of my concepts, however, does not mean that I do not know the individual. I could not even say that my understanding leaves the "this, here and now" out of consideration if I were not conscious of the individual. Whenever I know something, it is always and primarily an individual something to which I am present. But because I cannot seize the individual's reality in a single concept, I need many conceptual expressions to state what the concrete terminus of my cognitive encounter is. In this sense the abstract-conceptual expression of the terminus encountered by my act of knowing *divides* the original unity of this terminus into fragments.

In another sense abstractive understanding also establishes *unity* in the subject's field of presence. My understanding of a house is such that "all" houses are com-prehended in my understanding, not as individual concrete things, but as *essentially* like each other. In this way meanings which are essentially in agreement are put together as a specific region. For one who dwells "understandingly" in the world, the world is composed of such specific "regions of being," as the regions "tree," "house," "car," and "chair." The world is no longer chaotic, but reveals unity and interconnection when I dwell "understandingly" in it. My concepts are universal: they can be affirmed of all objects pertaining to a "specific region of being."

The Abstract Concept Is Not a Schematic Image

Empiricists, such as Hume, claim that, strictly speaking, there is no difference between the concept and the sense image. Every impression from without is wholly individual, an impression of *this* box or *that* box. If one asks by what right the one term "box" is used to indicate all those impressions, we answer that we do this because in our experience of *this* box and *that* box we acquire the abstract concept "box" and in our understanding we leave behind the *this* and *that*.

The empiricist, however, cannot agree with this answer. For him, our so-called abstract concept is nothing but an impoverished and weak image of individual things, in which all the striking features of individuality have simply faded away. All that remains is a vague schematic image.

It is undoubtedly true that our knowledge contains also a schematizing aspect. But a schematic representation certainly is not the abstract expression of a thing's essence. When man does not go beyond a schematic image, there obviously is no understanding. For example, an anthropology which would restrict itself to the orderly arrangement of schematic images of individual human beings could produce only trivial statements about man. The schematization of individuals produces only an individual image, it is not an abstract conceptual expression of what a thing is. Moreover, a theory about the schematizing aspect of human knowledge is impossible without a *concept* of schematization, and this concept itself is not a schematization.

5. PHENOMENOLOGY OF TRUTH

As soon as he makes explicit the implicit "affirmation" of reality which he himself is, the *existent* subject pronounces a judgment. The judgment expresses that a certain object "truthfully" and "really" *is* what it is said to *be*, and, at the same time, implicitly "says" that the object is *not* something else. In every judgment the copula "is" is used, and the subject who says "is," intends to express that what he affirms "truthfully" and "really" *is* this or that. "Truth," therefore, is traditionally defined as the agreement of the judgment with reality. This definition is hardly debatable. Any philosopher will subscribe to it, but the reason for this unanimity lies in the fact that this definition as such does not really say anything. As soon, however, as one asks what is meant by "agreement" and "reality," the opinions at once differ.

While accepting the traditional definition of the truth of the judgment, phenomenology refuses to separate the explicit saying of "is" in the judgment from the implicit saying of "is" which the *existent* subject himself is. The truth of the judgment is preceded by a certain "event": the "event" in which the judged meaning becomes meaning-for-the-subject, the "event" in which truth is "unveiled," becomes unconcealed. If this "event" is disregarded, one can hardly escape making truth the agreement with brute reality. But in that case all truth is talked out of existence, for the affirmation of agreement between judgment and brute reality presupposes that it is possible to compare the judged reality with the non-judged brute reality. The realism of the so-called "natural attitude" (Husserl), which divorces subject and world, inevitably leads to scepticism. As a matter of fact, this is what happened to Hume.

Hume's Intelligent Scepticism

Rejecting innate ideas, Hume held that all knowledge is knowledge of sense experience and begins with simple impressions. The knower, then, is a mere "recipient" of impressions, "messages" from a world in which he does not live. All the knower knows is impressions, that is, contents of consciousness, for Hume conceived the world as divorced from the knowing subject.

Before Hume, Locke had already stated that what the knower knows is the *ideas* themselves. Consciousness was conceived as a kind of locker in which contents of consciousness are stored. This locker was fully separated from the world from which it receives "messages." Hume took over this view from Locke: the knower knows the "phenomena," the subjective impressions in his interiority.

Until Hume, thinkers had tried to make use of the principle of causality to reach that which is hidden behind the phenomena, but according to Hume such an attempt is sheer nonsense. For the whole idea of causality, he argues, simply arises from the experience of regular succession: if we repeatedly see A happen after B happens, we subjectively expect that A will happen whenever B happens and end up by saying that A causes B "out there" in reality. But the affirmation of the existence of a cause "out there" and its real operation is beyond justification: justified affirmations can only be concerned with subjective impressions. Hume's contemporaries realized that his philosophy was a radical form of scepticism, for his position leaves no possibility to know "reality."

Hume's scepticism, however, is the inevitable and logical consequence of any mirror theory of knowledge. In such a theory the "real" world occurs as a world-without-the-subject. Such a world is a world of which the subject is not conscious and which he does not affirm. How, then, could the subject ever affirm such a world? Hume was the first thinker to see the ultimate consequences of the realistic theory of knowledge. Existing reality, that is, the non-affirmed and non-known world, brute reality, is beyond our reach as far as Hume is concerned. This kind of "scepticism" is a very intelligent kind of scepticism.

Truth as Unconcealedness

The truth of the judgment is preceded by a more original truth. The truth of the judgment presupposes that what the judgment expresses is "already" drawn from concealedness; it presupposes *alētheia* (Heidegger), the unconcealedness of the matter judged. This unconcealedness requires a certain "light." If only *things* existed, there would be no "light" and nothing would ever be true. The unconcealedness of things presupposes that man has gone beyond thinglike being in himself, that man is a certain "light" for himself. This "light" is a "natural light," that is, it is a "light" which is man's own essence ("nature"), the "light" of his subjectivity. As *existent* subject, man lets things be meaning for him, lets them dis-close themselves to him, he stands in truth as their unconcealedness.

With the necessary changes, the same holds for the untruth of the judgment. This untruth presupposes that the subject no longer stands in truth as unconcealedness, but stands in "semblance." Reality is then not fully concealed: it is dis-closed to some extent but, at the same time, deformed. The untrue judgment is the expression of standing in semblance.

Objectivity and Objectivism, Subjectivity and Subjectivism, Relativity and Relativism

From the preceding considerations it should be clear that the meaning about which the true judgment makes a statement cannot be conceived as an "in itself," as being, independently of man, what it is said to be. For otherwise one disregards the fact that the meaning has been constituted by the subject who lets things be for him. By letting things be meaning for him, man "originates" truth. This does not mean, however, that man, in "originating" truth, can proceed arbitrarily. In his saying of "is" man has bonds. He is bound to respect that which shows itself, that which is unconcealed. Man is not the lord of being but only its shepherd and guardian: his task is to let meaning appear as it is. He must "respond" to being (Heidegger).

Thus it should be evident that there continues to be a kind of "critical problem": by what criterion can I determine whether in saying "is" I let myself be guided by unconcealedness? How do I know whether my "seeing" is or is not merely a putative seeing? Before we consider this question, we must first clarify certain terminological points.

There is no reason why truth as unconcealedness should not be called *objective*. For people who defend an objectivistic view of objectivity, the objectivity of phenomenology is not sufficiently objective, for the subject has not been eliminated from the encounter which knowledge is. The subject's elimination, however, would destroy the encounter, i.e., knowledge itself, so that there could no longer be a question of objectivity in *any* sense.

Most scientists and also some philosophers reserve the term "objectivity" for that which is connected with the intentionality of positive science and which can be verified by anyone who assumes its standpoint. Objective in *this* sense obviously is not identical with the unconcealed: it is merely one or several regions of the unconcealed, for much more is unconcealed than can be verified by positive science.

Phenomenology is often accused of being *subjective*, in the sense of adhering to a subjectivistic concept of truth. This accusation certainly is false; phenomenology does not deliver truth to the subject's arbitrary choice. The knowing subject is a "seeing" on many levels, but on every level he remains bound. When the phenomenologist says that all truth is subjective, he simply means that truth expresses objectivity-*for-a-subject*.

The same line of thought applies to the term *relative*. The phenomenologist's statement that all truth is relative should not be interpreted in a relativistic way; the relativity of truth solely means that truth is absolute *in relation to* a subject.

These ideas lead to a correct understanding of truth's *historicity*. If the truth of the judgment presupposes that truth is unconcealed, then, on the side of the subject, it also presupposes the historical act by which man draws truth from concealedness. We will develop somewhat more extensively the historicity of truth and describe the essentially unfinished character of man-as-history and of his truth-as-history. First, however, we wish to make explicit the implication that truth is radically human. The history of truth began with the appearance of man in the cosmos, and the appearance of a new human being means the beginning of a new history of truth. Man knows only human truth; therefore, there was no truth before man was: before man existed, nothing was unconcealed from man.

At this junction the objection is often made that, before man appeared, there was truth-for-God. But what does

77

this mean? It certainly cannot mean that the unconcealedness of reality-for-God would be in agreement with the
unconcealedness of reality-for-man. Even if one admits
that to some extent man can enter into the reality-for-God,
it certainly could not have happened before the appearance of man, the one for whom both God and the reality-
for-God would be unconcealed. We realize, of course, that
such statements are indigestible for many people: the
entire history of Western thought manifests the claim of
placing oneself on the absolute "standpoint" of God in
speaking about truth and in this way assign a divine
guarantee to human statements. This pretension exists
openly in idealism, but in a disguised form it is also present in scholasticism.

The Essentialism of Scholastic Philosophy

Scholasticism sees reality as a collection of essences-in-
themselves, stored in a land whose discovery is never
mentioned. This view has its roots in Plato. The latter
introduced a separate world of necessary and universal
ideas in order to explain the necessity and universality
found in human knowledge. Plato conceived the being of
ideas as the only "really real" being and made the ideas
the prototypes of worldly realities. Ideas were conceived
as necessary and universal norms for the truth of things.
Concrete living man had nothing else to do but realize his
necessary, universal, immutable and eternal essence in the
changeability of time.

Plato's world of ideas was a world of pure "light." The
meaning spoken of by phenomenology, however, is not a
pure "light" but an admixture of "light" and "darkness,"
of unconcealedness and concealedness. The unconcealedness of meaning presupposes that the subject lets meaning be: at the moment when the subject sees meaning,

truth as unconcealedness issues forth. This moment is the beginning of a never-finished history of dis-closure. Meaning is never pure "light."

The Platonic idea, conceived as pure "light," actually is meaning whose moment of coming to light is "forgotten" and whose history of dis-closure is assumed to have been completed. But for such a finished result there is no room within knowledge as a genuine *encounter*, for in the *real* encounter with meaning the latter reveals itself as the semidarkness of unconcealedness and concealedness and, consequently, as a never-ending invitation to further disclosure by the subject. Plato, however, cut meaning loose from the encounter and placed it as an "in itself" of a purely ideal kind in a world of pure essences.

Aristotle relocated the essences in the real world, but he also implicitly conceived their "reality" as "in themselves." He did not restore them to the encounter with the knowing subject. Like the Platonic essences, the Aristotelian essences were conceived as an absolute "light," as in themselves necessarily, universally, immutably and eternally "true": they were held to be the norm of truth for the judgment. In this way there arose a picture of reality as a collection of essences, stored in a land of absolute "light," while the history of the birth of "light" failed to receive any attention.

This view underlies scholasticism's realistic philosophy of order, which assigns to each essence its proper place in brute reality. Man also, with his own essence, had a place in that order: below God, but above animals, plants and things. The place of the holy was above the beautiful, the beautiful above the useful, the useful above the agreeable, the common good above the individual good, and the soul above the body. Similarly, the essences of human acts were assumed to be what they are: necessarily, universally, immutably and eternally true "in themselves." The

79

essence of the marriage act, for example, was conceived as in itself necessarily, universally, immutably and eternally orientated to reproduction. This orientation was the "truth in itself" of the marriage act, the norm for every judgment about it. Natural rights and duties also were placed in the "totality of reality" as necessarily, universally, immutably and eternally "true in themselves" and, consequently, the norm of all statements.

This state of affairs led to a specific theory of ethical deeds: the concrete living man lives an ethically good life if he "reads" the essences and their essential order and conforms his actions to what he "reads." By doing this, he fulfills God's will. For scholasticism also located the Platonic ideas, as exemplars of the real essences, in God's intellect: by a command of his will, God realized these exemplars in his act of creation. Scholasticism, then, ascribed "truth in itself" to the essences, and this "truth in itself" was measured by, and derived from their being "true" in God's intellect. Insofar as man's true knowledge mirrored the "truth in itself" of the essences, man possessed God's view of things. In this way the essentialism, objectivism or realism of scholastic philosophy terminated in the claim to speak in the name of God.

An objectivistic philosophy exaggerates the bonds which hold man when he speaks about reality so much that truth is conceived as an absolute "initiative" of "objective" reality. The subject "humbly" withdraws as a "simple spectator": he is not involved in the "coming about" of truth. But in this way the "objective" reality is "objective"-for-no-one, so that no one can say anything whatsoever. The "humble" objectivist, however, continues to speak, but his "humility" turns into absolutism here: he ascribes what he says to the absolute "initiative" of "objective" reality. God's "created truth" is assumed to have the "initiative," but the subject cannot avoid thinking that he represents this "initiative."

It is not difficult to see that such a philosophy is dangerous because it eliminates all risks from man's search and
"origination" of truth. But, as we saw, it is the *existent*
subject who lets truth as unconcealedness "come to pass."
We will still see that, in doing this, the subject has no
guarantee whatsoever. While thinking that he gives expression to truth, he can easily express untruth. Objectivism buries this risk under verbiage. It elevates itself to the
absolutism of God's "created truth in itself": thus it can
declare anyone wrong who has at his disposal only his
seeking and groping for truth-for-man. It declares him
wrong "in the name of God." The objectivist does not even
need to enter into dialogue with anyone, for he is "one who
knows" the answers (Merleau-Ponty). But who does not
see that the objectivist does not really have God's "seeing"
of the truth at his disposal but only his own seeking and
groping subjectivity?

The Historicity of Truth

The fact that truth as unconcealedness refers to man as
a "light" is the first reason why truth must be called
historical. When man emerged from the cosmos, a "light"
began to shine in the darkness; the event of man's coming
to be as a subject meant that there was now a being
existing for itself, a conscious being in the world. At the
same time, things and the world began to be for this
being, for the subject is the "letting be" of things and the
world. Thus, the "moment" of man's emergence as a subject was equiprimordially the "moment of seeing," the
"moment" at which truth was born. In this sense truth is
historical.

Next, truth must be called historical because the subject's emergence is not a one-time event which occurred
when the subject first appeared in the cosmos. This emergence continues to occur whenever the subject transcends

any kind of "facticity." It is a never-finished event, for the subject reaches beyond the past of his "seeing" toward a future of "seeing." Knowledge, then, as dis-closure of meaning, is history, as the unity of past, present and future. This dis-closure is never "finished," so that the history of truth is essentially unfinished.

Finally, truth is historical because the birth of truth can come about only at a particular phase of the subject's personal history and in a particular phase of the collective history of mankind's search for truth in which every personal history is contained. For example, one who has barely started to think does not yet see the true essence of society, authority, love, justice, marriage, etc. One who has barely assimilated the first principles of physics does not yet have the necessary intellectual attitude to ask meaningful questions about nuclear chemistry. The same must be said with respect to mankind's collective search for knowledge or for that of a particular society. For instance, it is meaningless to discuss the truth of the ethical demand of support for widows and orphans with members of a society who have not yet reached the ethical stage where they can see that ethics demands the abolition of the practice of burning widows with their deceased husbands and of sacrificing children. In such a society the truth of a more profound ethical demand cannot yet "come to pass." That truth does not exist "there" at "that time."

Truth, then, is historical in a "triple" sense. But truth is also transhistorical. This point must be discussed now.

The Transhistoricity of Truth

Earlier in this chapter we saw that the relativity of truth must not be interpreted in a relativistic fashion: for truth is absolute but *in relation to* the subject. Hence, the recognition of historicity does not justify historicism, that is, the view that a truth is true today and that tomorrow it will no longer be true. Such a view would be a vulgar form of relativism, which is not even self-consistent. For whoever accepts this view as true must admit that the truth of this very view is true today but not true tomorrow; yet, by defending his view, he intends to express a "definitive" truth.

There are phenomenologists who reject "absolute truth" on the basis of truth's historicity. In our opinion, this rejection should be understood as a refusal to accept the absolute aspect of truth as isolated from its relativity. It is a rejection of the absolutism of truth, into which one is bound to fall if one does not do justice to the relativity inherent in truth's historicity. Both realism and idealism actually fail to do this.

Idealism cannot accept that "genuine" knowledge contains darkness. It conceives genuine knowledge as the perfect transparency of the Idea for the Spirit, the perfect self-possession of the Subject. It conceives truth as light without darkness, as "finished" truth. Such a view, however, falsely assumes that the history of dis-closure is completed. In the sense in which idealism understands the term, one must say that there is no "absolute truth," for idealism disregards the fact that the subject is situated in a particular historical "attitude."

The same applies to realism. According to realism, meaning is "true"-in-itself, an absolute light-in-itself. For such a light there is, of course, no room when knowledge is conceived as encounter. Meaning, as the *real* terminus of encounter, is a mixture of light and darkness. When meaning is conceived as an absolute light-in-itself, it is thrown out of the encounter, put down somewhere outside the real history of progressive dis-closure. Strictly speaking, such a claim makes all truth impossible; nevertheless,

83

the realist pretends to express truth, he pretends to speak "absolute truth," divorced from the relativity of his historical standpoint. For this reason the "absolute truth" of realism also must be rejected.

Absoluteness in the Life of Truth

The historicity of truth, however, does not mean that there is no sense in which one can speak of absolute truth. But absolute truth does not lie outside the history of the *existent* subject but within it, and precisely for this reason absolute truth is not a denial of relativity: absolute truth "comes to pass" in the subject's history.

Strictly speaking, every truth, no matter how personal, is absolute. When a degenerate mother stands before the corpse of the child she herself killed, the truth of her deed is indisputable, it cannot be denied, it can never be untrue in any phase of this truth's history. Even if no one else will ever know what she has done, she knows that she will never be able to agree with others who deny that she killed her child. Thus she affirms her truth not only in her own name but also in the name of all others. Her personal truth has absolute validity. At the historical moment of its birth, this truth acquired a transhistorical validity, and this validity is, in principle, intersubjective. The statement, then, that a truth is absolute in its relativity to a subject means that this truth is, in principle, transhistorical and intersubjective.

This aspect of absoluteness can also be expressed in the traditional terms "immutable" and "eternal," provided these terms are not understood in the sense in which Plato, Aristotle and Aquinas spoke of "immutable" and "eternal" truths as lying *beyond* history. Once a truth is "brought about" by man at an historical moment, this truth is immutably and eternally true. The term "eternal" does not mean here that there always have been or will be human beings, for whom this truth is true, but indicates that no one can ever deny this truth in any phase of his history. Similarly, the term "immutable" does not place truth outside history, outside the progressive dis-closure of reality. It remains possible that my "seeing" of today will reveal itself tomorrow to have been merely putative, so that my "truth" was mere "semblance." But if I really "see" today, my truth is immutable, even though it remains unfinished, capable of becoming more complete. Today's truth can be made more profound by, and integrated into tomorrow's truth.

Even so-called necessary and universal truths, such as those expressing the essence of man or things, are not "in themselves," divorced from the never-finished history of truth. These truths also are born, they presuppose the historical moment, the "fact" of their "coming about" by being "seen" by the human subject. This fact is not a necessary fact. In this sense even necessary and universal truths must still be called "conditional" or "factual" truths.

6. THE CRITERION OF TRUTH

That which is "evident" is indisputable and true. In "evidence" I experience the unconcealed, I "see." "Seeing," in the broadest sense of the term, that is, the immediate presence of the *existent* subject to a present reality, decides about truth. The subject, however, can not only "see" but also dream, desire and get lost in illusions. One who realizes that he has been dreaming when he thought that he "saw" something withdraws his judgment because now he really "sees." We know that we can make mistakes, but we can correct them only in the name of the truth which we subsequently "see." Obviously, it is meaningless to ask whether that which is evident, which we "see," is true; for true is that which we "see." The "critical problem," then, is not whether what we "see" is true, but where we can find a criterion to distinguish whether we are really "seeing" or merely dreaming, fancying and getting lost in illusions.

This question *must* be asked, for we contradict one another. One man thinks that the other lives in illusions, while the latter thinks that the former must be blind. Where are we to find a criterion to distinguish between the blindness of the one who does not "see" what is there and the illusions of the other who "sees" what is not there?

The "Fruitfulness" of Truth

Let us begin with a simple example. I have an instrument in my hands, of which John affirms that it is a pen while Peter claims that it is a screwdriver. John says that Peter must be dreaming, but Peter argues that John must be blind. How do I know who is right? In daily life one would say: "Let Peter use the instrument to fasten a few screws; then he will see." The philosopher expresses the same idea when he says that the criterion of truth is the fruitfulness of the subject's dialogue with reality. Things reveal what they are within this dialogue, if only because at a given moment the dialogue itself becomes impossible; reality becomes so overloaded with fancied meanings that it ceases to give answers, offers resistance or is destroyed. If I use a pen as a pen, my action results in writing; the dialogue is fruitful: the verification of the meaning ascribed to the pen does not lead to frustration or contradiction. True is that which is "fruitful."

The physical sciences make use of the same criterion. The physicist questions reality by means of a certain *a priori* view, an hypothesis. He does not accept his hypothesis as true until reality *itself* reveals itself as he views it in his hypothesis. If his hypothesis is wrong, his dialogue with reality comes to a halt: reality gives no answer, or is destroyed. His dialogue with reality shows itself unfruitful. If, for example, he questions a particular substance, "thinking" that it is gold, and it does not answer his questions as gold, the scientist knows that he was imagining things when he formulated his hypothesis.

The same applies to the human sciences, but here it is much more difficult to question reality because in many cases it is impossible to perform experiments. Truth in these sciences is discovered only with the greatest difficulty. Entire generations of thinkers may have to pass before it becomes evident that a certain view is false, because it brings the dialogue with reality to a halt. Orthodox Freudianism can serve as an example. Psychoanalytic practice showed that there are other dimensions to man than sex. A fruitful dialogue between the psychotherapist and his patient often became impossible if the therapist held fast to Freud's narrow framework of ideas.

To return to "ordinary" life, what the sciences try to express in a universal way the "ordinary man in everyday life" is assumed to "know" concretely. The human sciences try to capture man's ways of dealing with himself, his fellowmen, society and God in order to formulate general insights into these relationships. In everyday life, however, man "practices" these relationships on the basis of concrete insights into their reality. The more complex the situation is, however, the more difficult it is to disclose the objective meaning of reality. Thus man cannot escape from making mistakes in religious, social and political life, education, justice, mental care, etc. Very often his dialogue with reality has to continue for a long time before man realizes his error and sees that he was living in untruth. Sometimes an entire life or even a civilization has to fail before man recognizes the truth about himself, society or God.

In spite of his conviction that he often errs, man must act. He cannot escape "making a mess of it," and he experiences that others also cause misfortunes. He cannot even escape by doing nothing or having no opinion, for doing nothing also is doing something and having no opinion is also having an opinion. Mans hands are always dirty (Sartre). There is a kind of material sinfulness in every personal history, as well as in the collective history of a society and mankind itself. This kind of "sinfulness" inspires the philosopher to the greatest prudence and reserve, it teaches him to be modest and self-effacing when he forms his opinions.

"Fruitfulness" of the dialogue with reality is also the criterion of truth in religious matters. The statement that a religion is true does not mean that a religious group is in possession of theses expressing the truth-in-itself about God, for religious truth also is truth in relation to man. The claim that truth is truth-for-man holds in one particular way for physical truth and *in another way* for religious truth. Similarly, the "fruitfulness" of the dialogue with reality as the criterion of truth holds in one particular way for physical science and *in another way* for religious knowledge. The dialogue of the physicist is "fruitful" when the affirmation of a particular truth leads somewhere: it makes new physical questions possible, eliminates the frustration of "wrongly formulated" physical questions, takes away the inconsistencies of previously given answers—in brief, it means that the physicist can realize himself as a physicist. *In this sense* one can say that the true is the "useful."

The true is true for a subject-with-a-particular-standpoint; consequently, the fruitfulness or unfruitfulness of the dialogue with reality also lies within that region of reality that corresponds to that standpoint. The fact that, for example, a particular truth from an artistic standpoint is not fruitful for man's self-realization as a physicist does not disqualify artistic truth. It would be unthinkable, however, that a truth would be fruitless on every level of man's being and, nonetheless, a worthwhile truth.

These ideas apply in a specific way to the truth of religion. The criterion to distinguish the illusion of one from the blindness of the other in religious matters lies in the fruitfulness of religion for a specific way of man's self-realization. A religion is not true because it eliminates the frustrations of a wrongly formulated question of *physics*. But this does not mean that a religion can be true and, nonetheless, remain unfruitful on *every* level. A truth that is wholly fruitless, of no importance whatsoever for man's self-realization in any respect, cannot be distinguished from an untruth.

We make these remarks here to draw attention to the "dizziness" (Merleau-Ponty) of man's search for the truth about himself. A true religion reveals itself fruitful for man's self-realization, and an untrue religion is untrue because, and to the extent that, it does violence to man. It is easy to write this in the light of the above-mentioned examples from life and the sciences. We tacitly assume, however, that man is in possession of enough truths about himself to establish the fruitfulness of certain religious truths for his self-realization and the unfruitfulness of others. But where do we find the criterion for the truth about man? A religion which leads people to burn widows and sacrifice little children is inhuman, we say, and therefore untrue. Rightly so. A religion which rejects work, physical science and technology is dangerous for man's self-realization, we say, and therefore untrue. Right again: such a religion opens no future, does not free man, is unfruitful.

But who does not see that all this can only be said in the supposition that the truth about man implies man's *duty* of self-realization and the essential role which work, science and technology must play in this self-realization? One who does not make this supposition has no reason whatsoever to say that a religion which makes man's self-realization impossible is untrue. He will call such a religion fruitful because he has an entirely different view of man's "having to be." A religion which leads to the burning of the widows and the sacrifice of children, we say, is not fruitful but pernicious for man, if man is conceived as destined for his fellowmen, a destiny that is accomplished in love. But such a statement presupposes that the truth about man's "having to be" lies indeed in love: one who does not make this supposition cannot call the religion in question untrue.

"Deciding" About the Truth

In connection with the above-mentioned examples, is it right to speak of presuppositions or assumptions? Are not those "assumptions" really evidences, truths about man? While we do not intend to deny an affirmative answer to the last question, we would like to point out that this affirmative answer itself evokes many new and difficult questions. For the truth about man also is historical: it "originates," "comes to pass" and is "brought about" by man in his never-finished history of becoming conscious of himself. Man is not the "lord" but only the "shepherd" of this history. His becoming conscious of himself is a "letting be" of his essence, not an autonomous and arbitrary deciding about his essence. But what criterion is there for the truth about his essence? How can he distinguish illusions and blindness from real "seeing"?

The sceptics have a ready answer: "Never!" Tempting as this answer may be, it is a self-contradiction. If the sceptic is serious, he is convinced of his statement that man's essence is such that man never knows whether a thesis about this essence is true. But by presenting this statement as true, the sceptic intends to explicitate a true aspect of man's essence, thus contradicting himself.

How seductive is the standpoint of the objectivist! He has simply eliminated every possibility of arbitrariness from the history of truth: the essence of man "is" necessarily, universally, immutably and eternally "true"-in-itself. In becoming conscious of himself, man is bound to respect this essence-in-itself. The objectivist's "advantage," however, is an illusion. For, whether there is a truth-in-itself about man or not really does not matter here, because, in order to judge, the objectivist has only his own opinions at his disposal (Merleau-Ponty). And these opinions remain subject to error.

The truth about man's essence also must be "brought about," but what does this mean? Hitherto we have always understood this term as the "letting be" and "disclosing" of a reality that is "already." But is this *all* that must be said of man's being insofar as this being is a "having to be," a task to be accomplished? True, man did *not decide* to be a bodily being, free, etc., but he did *decide* to realize himself as a worker, he did decide to destine himself for his fellowmen, at least to the extent of not capriciously destroying the other's life, he did decide to realize himself as a pursuer of science, he did decide to abolish polyandry and to be heterosexual. With respect to these modes of "having to be," man's becoming conscious of himself, then, was not a becoming conscious of what he "already" was *in the same way* as the affirmation of being a bodily being is an affirmation of what man "already" is. The affirmation of those modes of "having to be" was a decision about the essence of man by which man has come to be.

Although this decision was not an arbitrary decision—

man is not the "lord" of his own being—it is very difficult to account for it. *We* can *now* affirm that by the above-mentioned decisions man opted for the truth of his authentic being. In a certain sense one can even say that, "not knowing beforehand" the right answer, man was forced to make a *decision*. Now that man has chosen, however, he can never deceive himself into thinking that he would just as well have been standing in the truth if he had decided to deny what he actually did choose. This means not only that man cannot go back upon his decision, but even more that he would destroy himself by reneging on his decision. Man would lose himself if he would no longer realize himself as a worker and a pursuer of science, if he were to opt for polyandry, or did not decide to destine himself for his fellowmen at least to the extent of not capriciously destroying the other's life. In the history which followed his decisions, it became evident that those decisions let the *truth* of his essence "come to pass": the continuation of man's dialogue with his own essence remained fruitful, his becoming conscious of himself in this way revealed itself as a "successful" becoming self-conscious.

We who affirm this *today* are convinced that, with respect to the truth about man's essence, man does not *arbitrarily* proceed in making those decisions: we do not think that others who do not make those decisions are just as "right" as we ourselves are "right." In our eyes, these others are still living on a subhuman level. If they wish to find the truth about their own essence, they will have to make the same decisions.

In all this, however, there remains a certain darkness and obscurity. What made man opt for the decisions he made? What criterion guides him when he says that certain decisions are fruitful for the truth about his essence? Is there, perhaps, as Heidegger suggests, a "resort outside man" which "decides" about the truth of man's essence, so that he is merely called to listen to its decisions in order to find that truth?

7. REASON AND SCIENCE

When we spoke of the "natural light" which the *existent* subject himself is, we were concerned with what an age-old tradition refers to as human "reason." This insight found expression in the "definition" of man as "rational animal." Today, however, one could say, it is difficult to defend this "definition." Is not existentialism characterized precisely by its struggle against "reason," *tout court?* One can relive this struggle in the works of Pascal, Kierkegaard, Newman, Scheler, and Blondel, the forerunners of existential phenomenology. Were not their works a desperate attempt to escape from the clutches of "rational," "scientific" and "objective" knowledge of man, in the hope of thus arriving at an "existential" experience of "concrete" human reality?

This kind of jargon is familiar. It is used in season and out of season, usually without much competence. It fostered the view that existential philosophers were in favor of some mysterious kind of irrationalism, against which "sound" thinkers were bound to protest in defense of philosophy as *the* science, the "science of all sciences." Now that the smoke of the early battles has cleared, however, it is evident that existential phenomenologists do not object to reason, *tout court*, but only to certain conceptions of reason which, in their opinion, overestimated or underestimated the power of reason.

"Enlarged Reason"

To what extent can existential phenomenology accept the qualifier "irrational"? What is meant by "enlarged reason" (Dondeyne)? These are the questions that concern us here. Existential phenomenology would have to accept the predicate "irrational" if this term did not have any other meaning than the one ascribed to it since Descartes: the mathematical and physical reason which operates with the "objective" categories of quantity. Only *that* reason is entitled to the qualifiers "rational," "scientific" and "objective." Thus all other modes of knowing would have to be called "irrational," for "rational" is reserved for mathematical and physical thinking.

Once this view is accepted one can understand why Pascal said that in the realm of metaphysics and morality "reason" can only lead to errors. Pascal did not mean that man cannot say anything about God and morality. He certainly can, but his words do not come from "reason"— mathematical and physical reason—but from the heart. The heart has reasons which "reason" does not understand.

The recognition that knowledge contained also "irrational" moments, was a distinctive gain. Nevertheless, this kind of knowledge continued to be considered less "objective" and less "scientific." This was a tacit admission of the Cartesian prejudice that reason should refer only to mathematical and physical reason. Objectivity was guaranteed by science; hence less objective and less scientific meant less "reason."

Phenomenology cannot accept this. Reason is the power to let objective meaning appear; objective is that which I "see"; hence objective reason lets any meaning whatsoever be, even if the latter cannot be expressed in terms of quantity. Reason must be understood existentially, that is, it must be seen as the "light" of *existence* itself, and this light discloses much more objectivity than scientism would have us believe. Reason "sees" much more than scientism believes there is to see. There is no justification for considering existentially understood reason—so-called "irrational knowledge"—less objective;

consequently, it is better not to speak of irrational knowledge but of "enlarged reason."

The Sciences

The phenomenological view of the positive sciences is in line with its view of reason. Reason is the power to let meaning appear, but this "letting appear" always takes place from a particular standpoint. Because the *existent* subject can occupy many standpoints, there are also many worlds. There is not one world-in-itself, not even one scientific world-in-itself, but as many specifically different worlds as there are specifically different standpoints of asking questions.

The importance of the subject's standpoint has not always been realized. For Aristotle philosophy was an encyclopedia of all sciences and contained both philosophical and nonphilosophical questions. The ideal of the new sciences which arose in the seventeenth century did not differ much from that of Aristotle. Under the guidance of Comte it hoped to reach the stage where it could "mirror" the whole of "reality" in one giant system of sciences, each of which would follow the method of physical science and contribute its building block. With incredible optimism it was assumed that all blocks would neatly fit together and constitute a single harmonious whole of "unified science."

This ideal of science, however, has proved idle. The men of science themselves began to realize that they, too, do not speak of a world-in-itself: the sciences speak of *human* worlds. Secondly, it became gradually evident that the physicist's typical way of asking questions is only one among many possible ways.

A science is this particular science and no other because it addresses this particular question and no other to reality. Just as only sounds occur in the world connected with my ears, so only the objects of a specific science are connected with the specific question asked by this science. Colors are meaningless for my ears, but it is nonsense to deny colors on the ground that I cannot hear them. A specific science is born when a particular question is critically and systematically taken up. But this question is contained as an original "interest" in *existence* itself. Let us explain the matter through an example.

Existence together with fellowmen contains an original psychological interest. In daily life people deal with one another in ways that are obviously psychological or unpsychological. The behavior of a judge toward a delinquent, a job applicant toward his interviewer, a teacher toward his pupil, a girl toward a boy, etc.—all those ways of behaving obviously are either psychological or unpsychological. But, one may ask, what is psychology?

We need not answer this question here. But, whatever psychology is, it must cultivate and develop the mysterious psychological "knowing" contained in my *existence* together with my fellowmen: psychology systematically and critically takes up whatever "interests" man when he obviously proceeds in a psychological fashion. In psychologically dealing with someone, I assume a particular standpoint, and this standpoint determines the direction in which the corresponding science of psychology develops into a science. If a science does not succeed in taking up the original attitude of asking questions, it will not be able to develop in such a way that its pursuers have the experience of acquiring the knowledge which they pursued by virtue of their original "interest." It will then be necessary to revise the fundamental concepts used in that science.

Through the original "interest" a particular region of being is demarcated, but this first demarcation is not at once so sharp that the region in question is clearly delineated from the rest. The explicitation of a particular question is not at once so sharp that the question is clearly distinct from other questions answered in other sciences. For example, as long as one thinks that the earth is the center of the universe because God became man on earth, one confuses the intention of astronomy with that of theology. The fact that the various "landscapes" of reality merge and constitute a *Gestalt* explains why an improperly formulated question can still receive some kind of answer. If a psychologist thinks that he should adopt the ideals of physical science in his science, he can still say something about a smile: he can describe it as a "contraction of the nostrils and the corners of the mouth, accompanied by a twinkling of the eyes." This is something, but it is not what makes the psychologist interested in the smile. It tells us what the smile is for the physicist, but a psychologist should be able to say something else about it.

No science can come into its own without experiencing one or more crises in its fundamental concepts. The revision of those concepts means a more faithful explicitation of the origin "interest," the standpoint of that science. At the same time, a particular region of reality is more sharply delineated. As long as a science does not fully take over the original "interest" which first led to its birth, the man of science will remain dissatisfied because he cannot fully realize himself as a pursuer of that science.

Finally, it should be evident that no science is entitled to prescribe its own method and language to any other science worthy of the name. A method which can guarantee the scientific character of one science can also produce just the opposite effect in a different science and spoil its scientific character. This happens, for example, if psychology is reduced to physiology.

Suggested Readings

Luijpen, *Existential Phenomenology*, Chapter Two.

John Locke, *An Essay Concerning Human Understanding*.

David Hume, *A Treatise on Human Nature*.

Edmund Husserl, "Philosophy as a Rigorous Science," *Cross Currents*, Vol. 6 (1956), pp. 227–246, 325–344.

Martin Heidegger, "The Essence of Truth," *Existence and Being*, ed. by W. Brock, London, 1949.

Remy C. Kwant, *The Phenomenological Philosophy of Merleau-Ponty*, Pittsburgh, 1963.

Joseph J. Kockelmans, *Phenomenology and Physical Science*, Pittsburgh, 1966.

William James, *Pragmatism*, Longmans, Green and Co., New York, 1907. Several paperback editions.

CHAPTER THREE

Phenomenology of Freedom

THE EMPHASIS we have placed on being-in-the-world should not be taken to mean that human *existence* is wholly static and lacks any dynamic dimension. To *exist* is not merely being-in-the-world but also being-"at"-the-world. The particle "at" has here a meaning similar to the one it has in the expression "being at it": it indicates that one is doing something. Man is not wholly fixed in his world, but is dynamically in it. His dynamism is not a thinglike process, however, but the dynamism of a subject who is free.

Freedom always expresses, negatively, a certain absence of determination and, positively, a certain autonomy. But both are aspects of one and the same reality, viz., man. In speaking about freedom, phenomenology adheres to these two senses. When the various human sciences spoke of man, they considered man to be "the result of" whatever forces are studied in a particular science: man occurred in economics and sociology as nothing but the "result" of economic and social forces, in biology as the "result" of biological processes, and in orthodox psychoanalysis as the "result" of all kinds of drives dwelling in the *id*. Man was considered to be "all kinds of things," but always as the "result" of processes and forces, which, as in physical science, were supposed to act unilaterally and deterministically. Thus man was conceived as just a thing, for of a thing one can say, in the strict sense, that it is the result of processes and forces.

1. SUBJECTIVITY AND FREEDOM

Existentialists and phenomenologists have always rejected the view that man is nothing but the result of processes and forces, for then man *himself* would be nothing, and this is not tenable.

To Be a Subject Is to Be Free

A thing can be fully explained in terms of its antecedents: its being is a being-result. One who knows everything about the forces acting on a thing, knows everything about the thing: it is merely a temporary point of rest in the evolution of the cosmos, it is nothing new with respect to the forces acting on it, it does not *itself* transcend its antecedents. The being of a thing is nothing but its belonging to the material cosmos.

The fact that a thing is nothing but a result means that the thing is necessitated, for determinism governs the world of things. The cosmic forces operate with necessity and give to the processes the constancy which the scientists formulate in their physical laws. The deterministic forces operating in the cosmos work "blindly": they do not have any knowledge of themselves as forces and of their results as results. Things are not for themselves or for other things. In short, the being of a thing is being a blindly determined result.

The statement, however, that things are not for themselves and for other things, that they have no meaning for themselves and for other things, can only be made if the totality of reality contains *more than things*. If there were nothing but things, there would be no meaning. Paradoxically expressed, if there were only things and processes, nothing would *be*, in the only sense which the verb "to be" can have, viz., being-for-man. But something *is*, there are things, processes and forces.

Once this point is understood, it becomes impossible to say that the totality of man, all that man is, is the blindly determined result of processes and forces. For man would then be a thing and, therefore, strictly speaking, nothing would *be*. But something *is*, thanks to the appearance of man in the cosmos. Man's being, then, cannot be called nothing but a result: being man *itself* also is something. True, man's being is *also* a result, *also* necessitated, *also* a part of the cosmos, but it cannot be *totally* result, necessitated, part of the cosmos, for otherwise nothing would be.

Subjectivity is the aspect of man's reality by virtue of which he rises above being the blindly determined result of processes and forces. With the appearance of subjectivity in the evolution of the cosmos, a breach occurred in the "darkness" of matter. Man as subject is the "natural light," the light through which something *is*, in the only possible sense of this term.

Freedom, we said, negatively expresses a certain absence of determination. It should be evident, then, that being-subject is being-free, for through his subjectivity man rises above his being-a-thing. If everything man is were the result of blind processes and forces, man would be a thing, and nothing would then be. Man's being-subject is a being-free as the "letting be" of the cosmos. Obviously, we are not concerned here with freedom as the quality affecting a human action or power. Freedom here refers to the *being* of man on the proper level of his manhood. The being of man as a subject is a being-free. It

101

is only on the basis of this more fundamental freedom of being that one can speak of freedom with respect to a power or an action.

Positively considered, man's freedom as a subject implies a certain autonomy. The being of man as a subject is a being-a-*self*. Man cannot be fully explained in terms of his antecedents; the being of man as a subject is a being "from himself," a being "original." As a subject, man is a "substance" and belongs to himself. But what is man *himself?* The answer admits no hesitation: man *himself* is an "I," a person. Thus a man's freedom as a subject must be positively understood as a certain autonomy of being, an independence, a belonging to himself as a "being of his own" because he is not merely the result of processes and forces. Scholastic philosophy reserved the term "subsistence" to indicate this autonomy of being. As a subject, a person, an "I," man "subsists."

To Be Free Is to Be Rational

The being of man as an "I" means a certain ontological superiority over the things of the cosmos. This superiority is the "natural light" through which man exists for himself and through which the world exists for man. It is the light through which there is objective meaning. The traditional term for this light is "the light of reason." Man's reason is the "locus" where objective meaning appears and the power to let it appear, and this "locus" and power evidently are the *existent* subject himself. To be a subject means to be free and, equiprimordially, to be rational.

At the same time, however, it should be evident that freedom has inescapable bonds. The subject reveals himself as freedom, and freedom discloses itself as reason, as the power to let meaning appear. But meaning is objective, and the light of subjectivity is an "objective" light, in the sense that meaning is not left to the subject's arbitrariness. As a "natural light," the subject lets reality be, but his "letting be" is bound to objectivity. *Existent* freedom, then, is equiprimordially an *existent* being-bound.

Let us stress once more that we are speaking here of freedom and objectivity in their most fundamental senses. There is no question here of freedom of action or of a power, nor of objectivity as a quality affecting a judgment. What we are referring to is precisely that which is the foundation of freedom of action or of a power and of the judgment's objectivity. It is man as subject who is this foundation.

2. Freedom as "Distance," as "Having to Be," and as "Project"

If being a subject is to be free, then the way one conceives the subject is crucial for the more precise description of the freedom ascribed to man. If the human subject is conceived as an isolated subjectivity, then man's freedom obviously must be called absolute. This is done by Sartre.

Absolute freedom, however, does not occur among men because the human subject is not an isolated subject. The "I" occurs only as involved in the body and the world, with which it is not identical. The "I" posits itself only as intentional and situated. The subject's ontological autonomy, then, is relative, for it simply is not what it is without the body and the world. The freedom pertaining to man as a subject is equiprimordially a bond. Freedom is not an "acosmic freedom," it is not the fully autonomous source of reality's meaning, for without this reality itself, subjectivity is not what it is. The "I" affirms itself only as involved in the reality of the body and the world. The "I's" self-affirmation, however, lies on a twofold

103

level, and the same holds for the affirmation of the reality in which the "I" is involved. It lies on the cognitive level and on the affective level: the subject is not only a *cogito* but also a *volo* (I will). The "I's" self-affirmation contains not only the *recognition* of the "I" as "I" and of reality as reality, but also a *consent* of the "I" to itself and, fused with it, to reality.

The terms "affirmation," "recognition" and "consent" refer here to the *implicit* "affirmation" which the *existent* subject himself *is* and which underlies his judgments and decisions. Savoring a good glass of wine, the ecstacy of the bride, the happiness of finding a long-sought truth, the emotion resulting from seeing a sunrise in the mountains—all these are examples of affective involvement in, and affirmation of reality. The "I's" consent to itself is fused with its consent to reality. The "I's" self-affirmation on the affective level means a certain fullness of being, a certain rest and peace, which may be called "happiness."

"Distance"

As self-affirmation, the "I" is positivity of being. On the *cognitive* level, however, the recognition of the "I" as "I" implies also negativity, the denial of the "I's" identity with anything the body and the world are: the "I" is not the All. Similarly, the cognitive affirmation of reality implies negativity, the denial that the reality of the body and the world is identical with the "I" and the denial of the identity of any particular reality with any other particular reality: no reality is the All, but any reality is a finite positivity of being.

On the *affective* level (the *volo*) *existence* also has both positive and negative aspects. *Existence* on the affective level—which Heidegger calls "mood" or "tonality"—is both a "finding oneself to be well" and a "finding oneself not to be well": the world is both a "home" and "alien to home." The subject's consent to reality is never unreserved: he can never fully "say" yes to any reality. Neither money nor sex, science nor power, health nor the Revolution—in a word, nothing fully satisfies man. The subject's affective yes to the world includes also an affective no. All fullness of being-man is equiprimordially emptiness, all satisfaction is infected with dissatisfaction, all peace, rest and happiness contain conflict, unrest and unhappiness. The "yes" within *existence* excludes absolute "nausea" (Sartre); the "no" makes absolute consent impossible. The world is my home, in which I long for a better fatherland.

The negativity involved in the subject's affirmation of, and consent to himself and to reality is sometimes called "distance": the subject distances himself from unreserved affirmation and consent.

"The Being for Whom in His Being This Being Is at Issue"

When Heidegger wishes to point out that man is not just a thing among other things but a subject, a person, he calls man the "being for whom in his being this being itself is at issue." A thing is not concerned with its being: it lies, as it were "crushed upon itself." A man, however, is not bald just as a billiard ball is smooth, he is not ill just as a cauliflower is rotten, he is not a hunchback just as a willowtree is gnarled, for man is concerned with his bald pate, the malfunctioning of his organism, his misshapenness. He has a relationship with what he is, and he has this relationship as a subject. Heidegger expresses this by saying that *Dasein* (*existence*) has a "relationship to being" which is "an understanding of being." It is this which constitutes what man *essentially* is, what makes

105

man's being differ from that of a thing. For this reason Heidegger says that for man *in his being* this being itself is at issue, thereby excluding that there would merely be question here of something accidental.

It is in the relationship of man as a subject to what he is, then, that there exist the above-mentioned positive and negative moments on both the cognitive and the affective levels. Nothing of all this is found in a thing. A thing does not have a relationship to its own being, it lies "crushed upon itself"; it cannot ask questions, wonder, be bored, sad or anxious, hope or despair.

Freedom as "Having to Be"

Man's freedom, phenomenologists say, is a "having to be." Let us see what this expression means. Affectively, as we saw, the subject distances himself from reality. While the subject also undeniably consents to reality, the reserve or negation affecting this consent cannot be annulled. No experience of value is such that the subject's yes is definitive and not also permeated with a no. This applies to every level of *existence*. For example, to the extent that an economic, social or political system has a certain value, man can consent to them and also to himself as an economist, a sociologist or a politician. But this consent is never such that it escapes all negativity. In this sense one can say with Sartre that man is a "hole in being." Man is never finished, whether as an economist, an artist, a philosopher or a physician, etc. Because man's yes can never be definitive, he must continually stretch himself forward to a new future. Man as a subject is not only a "natural light" but also a "natural desire."

All this indicates what phenomenology means when it calls the being of man a "having to be." Man is a task, a task-in-the-world. As long as man is man, his being is, and is essentially, a task. Man is never "finished," for a finished task is no longer a task. True, man can disregard the tasklike character of his being-in-the-world, but he then disregards himself as man. He then gives himself the mode of being of a thing: for a thing, being is not a task because it is not a subject, not free.

Freedom as "Project"

Man's being cannot be a task if his being does not include any potential. It should be evident, however, that this potential exists. Man, it is true, "finds" himself as "already" merged with a particular body and as "already" involved in a particular world. He finds himself as an American, a Jew, intelligent, cripple, a worker, emotional, ill, rich, fat, etc. All this constitutes what he "already" is, his past or, in present-day terms, his "situation," his "facticity."

This facticity means that man is, up to a point, "fixed." Certain possibilities are excluded by it. An American, for example, can never realize himself as a Frenchman but at most as a frenchified American; a cripple cannot realize himself as a mountain climber; one whose IQ is 80 cannot realize himself as Secretary of Health, Education, and Welfare. There is, however, no facticity which does not include some possibilities. If the determinations which make a man dumb, ill, fat, a worker or an American did not include any possibilities, he would not be *really* ill, fat, a worker or an American.

This statement applies to any facticity whatsoever. For example, I am never merely factically ill: my actual illness always includes possibilities. I can use my illness as a means to raise myself above those who never experienced illness, I can seize it as an opportunity to revolt against God, to become the radiant center of attraction in the

107

family or to tyrannize my surroundings. Any illness which does not include any possibilities is not a real illness.

We should keep in mind that the possibilities of which there is question here are *real* possibilities, they are based on certain specific actualities, and not to be confused with purely logical possibilities, the mere absence of contradiction between two terms. Similarly, the subject's potential being is not like the passive being-possible of mere things, to which something "can happen." Likewise, they should not be conceived as little plans which one can drop if he likes. The ability-to-be of which there is question here is an *existentiale*, an essential characteristic of man.

Human *existence* is the unity-in-opposition of factical being and potential being, of "already" and "not yet," of past and future. The term *project* is reserved to indicate this unity-in-opposition which man is. Man does not lie "crushed" in his facticity, but has elbow room, the leeway of his potential being.

Man's being, however, is a being-in-the-world; therefore, his potential being is a being-able-to-be-in-the-world. To every possible way of *existing* there corresponds a possible meaning of the world. The project which man is, is equiprimordially the project of his world.

Meaning as "Direction"

On the basis of the potential being contained in any factical meaning, it is possible to give a more profound sense to the term "meaning" than that of "appearing reality." Meaning reveals itself as "direction." For example, the factical meaning of the world for a college graduate contains many references to possible modes of *existing* which are, as it were, the "direction" his *existence* can take in the world.

The statement that for "man, in his being, this being itself is at issue" also assumes a new and more profound sense: it now means that for man his possibilities and those of his world are also at issue. Man is always "ahead" of himself and his world because of the leeway of potential being implied in his facticity. This leeway indicates the "direction" in which his *existence* can go. Note that this potential being is a potential of the *subject*. Man's possibilities are *his own*. To a thing something can "happen," but its various possibilities cannot be called possibilities of the thing *itself* because the thing is not a self. Man, on the proper level of his manhood, is "master of his situation," and holds his possibilities in his own hands. The project man is, is a *self*-project.

Man's being-a-project is not like a "little plan" which he can discard if he so wishes, but is an essential characteristic of man. In his own way Sartre expresses this idea very aptly when he points out that man "is not what he is but is what he is not." Man is not what he is (already), his facticity, for facticity leaves him the leeway of his being-able-to-be; at the same time, man is what he is not (yet), a being-able-to-be.

If man as project is called "freedom," there is no stringent reason why one should reject Sartre's statement that man is "doomed to be free." This expression means that there is question here of an essential characteristic which man cannot discard. Freedom as project, however, is not absolute but relative because it is connected with a particular factical situation, and this situation implies certain possibilities while excluding others. I am free, for example, to realize myself as a classical philologist, but this mode of potential being is implied only in the facticity of a college major in classics and not in that of a physical education major. I am free to realize myself as a mountain climber, but not on the basis of a facticity which makes

109

me a cripple. The situation, then, binds and limits me in many ways, and it is only within these bonds to my situation that I am free. In Heideggerian terms, the project which I am is a "thrown" project.

3. TO BE FREE IS TO BE ETHICAL

Freedom and being-ethical are often seen as opposites. Freedom is then conceived as being without bonds, and being-ethical as being bound by laws that are "there." In such a view the opposition is, of course, inevitable. But the view is primitive, for the assumption that freedom is being without bonds cannot be justified; moreover, this view leaves the origin of the moral law in darkness. Even if freedom is conceived as "selfhood," there remains a certain opposition between being-free and being-ethical as long as the moral law is conceived as a norm which is "there," that is, imposed from without on our freedom. There is opposition between a personalistic view of man and a legalistic concept of ethical obligation.

Legalism—the view that morality is nothing but willingness to obey the externally imposed law—favored an impoverished and even pharisaic pursuit of the moral ideal. If the good or evil of a human action depends solely on the agreement or disagreement with the law, then the attitude or mentality of the acting subject does not matter, and a purely external compliance with the law suffices to speak of a good action. Such a view fosters self-complacency and pride; one need not make any self-reproach, for one has acted "according to the rule." Moreover, there is then a ready-made criterion to judge others, viz., the external agreement or disagreement of their actions with the law. Observing that the other's actions deviate from the law, one has every reason to "wash one's hands in innocence" and to "thank God that one is not like him." This is pharisaism.

When moral life is conceived in a legalistic fashion, moral education can only appeal to fear of the consequences of one's failure to observe the law. There can be no question of a moral *ideal* from which one could derive the strength to overcome obstacles: the law is conceived as imposed from without and, consequently, the law itself has to provide the motive for its observation. This motive is found in the threat of penalties. Moral educational value is thus attributed to the law itself and even to mere "regulations."

Legalism was not only a prevailing mentality in a certain period of history but is, more especially, a perennial temptation, against which the authentically moral man must always struggle. Later we will see that this struggle implies a refusal to be satisfied with a minimum, to substitute a processlike observance of the law for moral creativity, a refusal also to sacrifice the progressive character of moral life to the mere abiding by formulated rules.

Sartre's Deathblow to Legalism

Sartre did away with legalism by a very simple expedient: he denied the existence of general norms and values. There are no universal norms because there is no God who has written such norms in heaven. Sartre finds it very "annoying" that there is no God, but if He does not exist, someone has to invent values. Life has no *a priori* meaning: man has to give meaning to it by inventing values.

Values, he holds, do not exist in themselves and have no meaning in themselves, by which they can impose themselves on the will, but they always presuppose the subject. Man never encounters pre-given values and goals when he enters the world. Thus freedom is the *only* foundation of values: nothing, absolutely nothing justifies the acceptance of this or that particular value or scale of values. My freedom is the groundless ground of all values.

The firm anchorage which traditional Christian morality has always offered simply does not exist according to Sartre. There are no signs through which man knows what he ought to do. Sartre illustrates this point by means of an example. In a prisoner of war camp he became acquainted with a Jesuit, whose father had died young and left the boy behind in great poverty. He was able to attend a boarding school, but its directors continually reminded him that he was a charity case and denied him the scholastic distinctions which he deserved. Later, he experienced disappointment in love, and in his military service also everything went wrong. Finally, he began to see in all this a sign from God: he was called to work for the triumph of religion. For this reason he had become a priest. But, according to Sartre, the man himself and himself alone evidently gave to the "sign" the meaning he wished to ascribe to it. Why didn't he interpret the "sign" as an indication that he should become a carpenter? Obviously, because he did not wish to become a carpenter. Thus he himself was fully responsible for his decision.

Even if there were general norms, Sartre adds, they would be wholly useless for man. During the war one of his students came to seek his advice. Should he go to England to join the Free French Forces or remain at home and support his aging mother? Triumphantly Sartre remarks that there is no system of universal moral norms which can answer this question. Christian morality preaches love and recommends the hardest way—but what is love? Serving France or supporting a mother—which is hardest? Kantian morality says that man may never treat his fellowman as a mere means but must

112

always consider him an end. But he who remains with his mother treats his fellow-combatants as means, and he who joins them treats his mother as a means. Therefore, universal norms of morality are useless. Even if there were a God, that would not make any difference in this respect: "You are free, choose, that is, invent."

The careful reader can hardly fail to notice that all kinds of questions are confused here. For Sartre there are no values "in themselves"; *therefore*, man is the absolute source of values. God did not write any general laws "in heaven"; *therefore*, there are no general laws. No moral system can indicate what ought to be done here and now; *therefore*, all systems are superfluous. No sign from heaven guarantees man that his actions are good; *therefore*, man must invent his own norms in absolute autonomy. This is confusion confounded and gives Sartre all the desirable elbow room he needs for his own view of morality.

A Universal Norm in Spite of Everything

Nevertheless, according to Sartre, there exists a universally valid morality and a universally valid norm. This norm is freedom. Dostoevski said that, if God does not exist, everything is permitted to man. "Indeed," says Sartre, "this is the starting point of existentialism." In absolute autonomy man must create values, invent norms and choose his morality. He can choose whatever he wishes as long as he chooses freely. Freedom is the universal norm.

Anticipating the objection that there is no universal norm, Sartre adds that there is a universal norm, but it is not written in heaven: the universal norm is the expression of man's essence, his absolute freedom. People who depreciate their absolute freedom by looking for heavenly

signs as a guarantee for their actions or who point to their
passions as an excuse for their deeds are in bad faith: they
live inauthentically, immorally, for they disregard what
they are—absolutely free. They are cowards and rascals!!

But may man not choose freely to live in bad faith? No,
says Sartre: he who wishes to live in bad faith, disregards
the *truth* of his essence, which consists in freedom as
absolute autonomy. The being of man is a "having to be"
in the bond of his essence's objectivity. For Sartre this
essence is absolute autonomy. Certain ways of choosing
are based on the truth of his essence, others disregard this
truth. Man, therefore, can do good and evil. The truth of
his essence imposes itself upon him as an obligation. For
this reason the objectively universal moral law is at the
same time also subjectively universal, it imposes an obligation on every man, according to Sartre.

The Ethical Law and Conscience

Is being-ethical a "standing under the law"? Must the
ethical law be called a law that "is already there"? Is there
opposition between freedom as "selfhood" and the law?
Are there laws which hold for everyone, always and everywhere? Let us see to what extent it is possible to
answer these questions on the basis of the insights we
have acquired into freedom.

Man's being-a-subject, we said, is the basis of his "having to be," because the subject can never fully consent to
his facticity. This same subject is also a light for himself
and the world. This light is an objective light and, as
such, bound by the objectivity of *existence.* Man is a being
for whom his being itself is at issue, the *objectivity* of his
being is at issue for him; he is characterized by "understanding of being."

If, then, the acting subject realizes himself in the

world, it goes without saying that awareness of being bound by the objectivity of his own essence accompanies man in his action. For man himself *is* this awareness. The realization that he is bound by the objectivity of his essence forbids man to make fanciful assertions about himself or to say anything which a particular government or a particular tradition wishes to see recognized as "truth." This same awareness also plays a role when man acts, for in acting perhaps most of all man can recognize or disregard the truth of his essence. In his actions man is accompanied by his awareness of the fact that he is bound by the objectivity of his own essence, and this awareness is man himself.

Realizing that the subject who is bound by the objectivity of his own essence is the same subject whose being is a "having to be," we must now say that the *existent* subject in his "having to be" is bound by the objectivity of his essence, by what he really is. If, then, it is true that, as we will see, the subject-as-*existence* essentially implies a "destiny for other subjects-as-*existences*," then the objectivity of man's own manhood obliges him never to destroy the others' subjectivity. People who lived authentically preferred to sacrifice their lives rather than disregard the objectivity of their essence through their actions.

We are speaking here of what is traditionally called "the ethical man." The "understanding of being," previously mentioned in a broader context, reveals itself here, in a more restricted framework, as what is traditionally called "conscience." And because of the fact that man himself is this "understanding of being," man's being must be called a "being-conscientious."

Since the beginning of authentic philosophical thinking, philosophers have tried to explicitate and conceptualize the ethical dimension of man. Their intention was not to determine what the individual ought to do or to omit in

115

individual cases, but they were concerned with the *essential* moments of man's being as a "having to be" in bond to the objectivity of his essence. Their endeavors resulted in objectively universal norms—norms, therefore, which are not written in heaven but "impressed in the hearts of men." The fact that these laws and norms, once they have been formulated, can begin to live a kind of isolated existence, divorced from their source, can become an occasion for the worst possible forms of objectivism and legalism.

Objectivism in Ethics

In legalism, the moral law is, as we saw, conceived as "already there" and "imposed from without." Norms are conceived as norms-in-themselves. It is this view which is denied—and rightly so—by Sartre and Merleau-Ponty. But they express themselves very badly when they formulate their denial as a rejection of "general norms." What they really intend to deny is the idea that general norms exist in themselves, and for this reason these two philosophers are subsequently able to admit again a general norm. For Sartre this norm is absolute freedom, for Merleau-Ponty it is the recognition of man by man. Both thinkers rightly oppose the objectivism which legalism surreptitiously introduced in its affirmation of the objectivity of general norms.

Truth must be "brought about" by the subject, as we saw in Chapter Two, and this statement applies also to the truth of ethical norms. The subject is free because he is not the blindly determined result of cosmic forces. In this sense truth originates in freedom. This does not mean that the subject arbitrarily decides about truth, but it does mean that general ethical norms are born in history, that their truth is "brought about" by the freedom which the subject is. When at a given place or in a given time the truth of an ethical norm is not "brought about," then we must say that this norm does not exist there and then. In other words, ethical norms also are objective-*for-a-subject*.

In his opposition to objectivism Sartre claims that, even if general norms "were written in heaven," they could not help man. For he would still have the task of "deciphering" those norms in order to make them meaningful. Sartre clarifies this assertion with the above-mentioned example of the situation facing one of his students during the war and observes that no system of general norms can give any answer. Universal norms, therefore, even if they existed, would be entirely useless. "You are free, choose, that is, invent."

Sartre is right on one point: "norms written in heaven," that is, norms-in-themselves, obviously cannot help man. General norms have to be "deciphered," that is, their truth must be "brought about." But when he advises his student to choose in freedom either to support his mother or to join the Free French Forces, he actually has already made use of a general norm by simply disregarding a third possibility: his student could have decided to become a collaborator or a traitor. For Sartre this possibility does not even deserve mention because, by virtue of the general law that one may not destroy the subjectivity of one's countrymen, it was already excluded for him. Thus the universal moral law is not entirely useless.

Next, it is a mistake to think that a *universal* norm should be able to indicate how man must act in his *concrete* situation. The understanding of what should be done here and now arises from the encounter of man's moral "having to be," the ethical ideal which man essentially is, with the concrete situation. The conviction that he is destined for the other is not enough to let man know whether this particular deed is such that it destroys or fosters the other's subjectivity. Thus he has to consider

117

the deed itself and the situation in which it is done. The claim that an insight into the way a particular deed affects the other's subjectivity can be derived from the general law is tantamount to the assertion that general esthetics enables the artist to conclude what he must paint on *this* wall and how he should do it. In this sense the acceptance of general norms does not itself guarantee and justify any moral choice. Accordingly, universal moral norms do not suffice when man must make a moral decision.

Universal laws do not suffice for an authentically moral life. An added reason for their insufficiency is that they do not explicitate moral life as an ideal of being-man. In particular is this the case when they are negative and express moral demands in a minimal fashion. An authentic moral life implies on the part of the subject an ever-renewed application to a task that is never finished, for man is a "having to be" and therefore never finished.

In an authentically moral life, then, there is always progress. This progress does not consist in an ever more accurate observance of increasingly more sharply defined laws, but in a conscience which forever is more clearsighted and forever more faithfully executes an ideal that has never been reached. Moral life also has its geniuses and inventors. They do not need minimalistically defined laws because, in their personal endeavor to attain the ideal, they accomplish more than those laws prescribe.

For an authentic moral life, the "prevailing" laws are even a danger. Any moral life begins with the almost processlike observance of the laws which "prevail" in a society. The violation of these laws is punished in an almost processlike fashion. The danger in this is that moral life will never go beyond a kind of automatic functioning under the law, thus giving rise to a legal fixism which depreciates any authentically moral life.

On the other hand, it would be wrong to deny the value

of the law, understood as a kind of moral facticity of society. Yet this is often done on the basis of a mistaken moral idealism, which thinks that the moral ideal can be reached without "passing through the law." This attitude can be compared to the mistake of people who experience the attraction of authentic, personal philosophizing, form a "circle," place themselves above every "ready-made truth"—or dogmatism, as they say—and then seriously think that in this way they can produce a valuable philosophical achievement. They invariably end up below the level of the so-called "ready-made truth." In a similar way, those who place themselves above the moral law with an appeal to the personal character of the moral ideal end up below the law, below the minimum. Man needs the law as a "crutch," at least in hours of waning idealism, discouragement and weakness, to remain steadfast and produce at least the minimum. The alleged need to reject the moral law of a society as mere facticity in favor of an untrammeled personal morality is an anthropological mistake. Just as the subject is not without a body, so also the moral subject is not without a "moral body." This is a point that the champions of freedom should never forget.

The "Body" of Conscience

Obviously we are concerned here only with the personal conscience, the mature conscience of man on the proper level of his being-man. This conscience, however, has certain infrastructures, a biological, psychological and sociological foundation, the reality of which has been disclosed principally in the past few decades by the corresponding sciences. Specialists in these sciences managed to show that the so-called "lack of conscience" is often the result of serious disturbances on an infrahuman level; such as from lack of affection during early childhood. The

119

integrity of an adult conscience presupposes that these infrastructures underwent a favorable development. This is not surprising, for man's subjectivity is an embodied-subjectivity-in-the-world. It would be wrong to identify rudimentary and primitive forms of conscience with the adult conscience—we do not say the *conscience of an adult* but an *adult conscience*, for in many so-called adults the conscience has not developed beyond one or the other of its rudimentary or primitive forms.

The personal conscience rises above its infrastructures and primitive forms of conscience. Without being identical with them, however, it continues to presuppose these infrastructures, as should be evident also from the many "diseases of conscience." Freud caused great confusion by simply identifying the personal conscience with those infrastructures. This, however, does not give anyone the right to reject what Freud "saw." Freud must not be refuted but complemented.

The same applies to the sociologistic conception of conscience. For social determinists, such as Lévy-Brühl and Durkheim, personal conscience is nothing but the product of a society's actually prevailing views, the sediment of socially accepted ways of doing things. Thus there can no longer be question of a *normative* morality but only of a "science of mores." The idea of obligation is either eliminated or reduced to the "obligation" to respect the established norms.

Why, however, would respect for those norms be an *obligation?* A "way of doing things" simply means that there exists a certain facticity. The claim that I am *obliged* to conform with this facticity has an entirely different meanings. On the proper level of my manhood I am the one who endeavors to evaluate the suggestions contained in my "social body," the facticity handed down to me, and as long as I have not done this, my conscience is not yet, in the full sense of the term, *my* conscience. Sociologism completely disregards the personal initiative by which I "place myself at a distance" from established facticity. In its stead, sociologism puts the "collective conscience," the established social infrastructures. While the personal conscience is always based on social infrastructures, it cannot be reduced to them.

Evil

If the ethical moment *par excellence* of man's "having to be" is his destiny for his fellowmen, then man's refusal to execute this destiny is ethical evil *par excellence*. Conscientious people are always aware of the possibility of evil in their lives, and for this reason they "examine their conscience." But what does this mean and how should it be done? When he examines his conscience, man tries, as it were, to "catch" himself. It is very important, of course, that he try to catch himself where he *really* can be found, and that is not in an interiority isolated from the world *à la Descartes*, but in the world.

The *real* ethical level of a person or a society is not determined by ethical "principles." The humanity of a society is not identical with the principles embodied in its constitution, the texts written in gold on its monuments, or the slogans of its orators. The loftiest "principles" will not absolve a person or a society if they do not become embodied in the world, in "the market place" where man deals with man.

Because he is conscious of his personal infidelity to the moral ideal, the authentically moral man is inclined to be almost apologetic for the sublimity of his principles. He realizes that his principles are clean, but not his hands. Nevertheless, he will have to defend his principles, for truth, including moral truth, is, in principle, intersubjec-

121

tive. Unfortunately, however, truth is not *de facto* always intersubjective. Since a society of persons can only exist on the basis of a common truth, life becomes increasingly more difficult when moral demands are frequently reneged upon in practice by those who see and recognize the objectivity of these demands. For, when this happens, how will those who do not yet "see" learn to "see?"

Objective Sinfulness

If man were an isolated subject, locked up in himself and separated from the world, life as a "beautiful soul" (Hegel), unstained by evil, would be possible. But man lives in the world, in history, among his fellowmen, and this means that the "absolute" good is beyond him.

First of all, man causes evil in the world because he does not perfectly know what he is doing. While *intending* to give meaning and harmony to history, man will *de facto* also cause meaninglessness and disharmony. Man knows what he does but, at the same time, he also does not know it. Oedipus did not wish to murder his father and marry his mother, but he did. The city of Athens did not wish to kill Socrates, but it did. Well-meaning parents do not wish to make life impossible for their children by exaggerated discipline, but many of them do. Those parents who abstain from exaggerated discipline do not wish to leave their children without any authoritative guidance and disorientated, but many of them do. The bearers of public authority in a society do not wish to prevent the community's development toward a new future by silencing advocates of progressive ideas, but some of them do. Others who do not silence the progressives in order to leave room for the new future, do not wish to offer opportunities for corrupting the younger generation, but it can happen that they do. Leaders of a church do not wish to irritate its members or make the church ridiculous in the eyes of outsiders, but some of them do.

Secondly, man brings evil into the world because his action also produces side-effects which he rejects and does not approve. One who creates meaning within a particular system of meanings must be resigned to the fact that he creates meaninglessness and evil within another system. For example, one who extinguishes a fire on the upper floor of a building cannot prevent the lower floors from being flooded. One who strips backward people of their pseudo-religiousness will make it impossible for many of them to give any structure to their lives. One who does not destroy an enemy having fifty ICBMs when he still has the power to do so, must accept the possibility that ten years later he will be confronted with an enemy having five hundred of those missiles.

The question at issue here receives its full importance in the realm of politics. It is ridiculous to object to the "evil" of flooded lower floors in the case of fire on the upper floors because this "evil" is not too serious and can easily be repaired. But in matters political the situation is entirely different. The politician who is not a barbarian will act with an appeal to the ethical ideal. He will have to exercise authority and use force. He intends to defend his fellowmen against "evil" and must be ready to make victims in their defense. But this means that it is always possible to oppose him on the basis of the ethical ideal: he is making victims. But what does this resistance mean? Those who resist the making of victims intend to establish meaning and harmony in history. But when *they* let their intention enter the world to defend fellowmen against "evil," they must exercise authority and use force. They, too, will make victims, other victims. It cannot be denied, of course, that they create meaning in history. But the absolute good is impossible. In reality, they do not oppose "evil," *tout court*, for they *also* create evil. Man cannot liberate himself from this evil by absolutely abstaining from any violence. For one who renounces all violence in a world in which violence "reigns" makes himself an accomplice of those who profit from the existing violence.

In the realm of politics especially it is true that a meaning which is good in a certain context can be seized by others, placed in a different context and orientated to a future which was precisely not intended by the original giver of meaning. An example is the reproach addressed to Pope Pius XII that he did not protest against the persecution of the Jews in the Third *Reich*. His hands would have been clean, so it is said, if he had fearlessly preached the "principles of justice" in which he believed. But may man preach justice and disregard the fact that his sermon will produce victims? The Dutch Cardinal de Jong did protest the persecution; it did not alleviate the sufferings of the Jews but caused new victims. Man sometimes cannot escape a situation in which he has no other choice than to "select" his victims.

From all this it should be evident how reprehensible critics are when they ascribe the objective evil in history to the personal evil intentions of those who have to act and who, even by not acting, act. Politics is not *per se* diabolical and politicians are not *per se* barbarians. But the absolute good is impossible.

Thirdly, man's involvement in the objective structures of the economic, social and political world makes a pure conscience impossible as long as these structures *also* embody murder and slavery. Murder and slavery are institutionalized in tyrannical colonial systems, inhuman economic orders as well as the intolerant fanaticism of both pseudo-religiousness and certain forms of atheism. I did not create the world's economic system, in which 17% of mankind owns more than 80% of the world's wealth. I am against the system because it offends my "principles." But this does not mean that my hands are clean, for in a certain sense I "agree" with the system by living off it. The evil described here is not my personal wickedness. I cannot cleanse myself by withdrawing my hands in order to live with "clean" principles and "good" intentions in the "interiority" of my conscience. One who withdraws his hands leaves everything as it is: he becomes guilty of the personal "sin of omission." His "interior" life is no alibi for the catastrophes of history: there is no pure conscience in a rotten world. The ethical man is a task-in-the-world, a task which is always also a failure.

4. FREEDOM AS TRANSCENDENCE

When psychologists, pedagogues and moralists speak of freedom, they usually refer to freedom of action. In the preceding sections we have discussed more fundamental senses of the term "freedom." The sciences in question do not deny these senses, but are less immediately interested in them. Let us consider now this freedom of action.

Human Action Is Not a Process

The character of the freedom proper to human action should be evident now: man's free action is not a deterministic process, no mere discharge of forces. Man's action, on the proper level of his being-man, is the execution of the self-project which man is. As a subject, man possesses a certain autonomy of being with respect to the processes and forces acting upon him, and this autonomy reveals itself most clearly in the human action.

The reason is that an action is human insofar as man *himself* is its origin. The result of the action is a meaning which is "new" in reference to the forces acting upon

125

man. When, for example, John bumps into Peter and
makes him fall, the meaning of Peter's fall cannot be
disclosed through mechanics, by calculating the force
with which John bumped into him. Peter's position in
space is "new" in reference to that force because of the
attitude which Peter *himself* assumes toward his fall.
Because man *himself* acts, his action is not a process. To
the extent that man's activity is not a process, it is free.

Perhaps it is better to emphasize here that the human
action always only *co*-originates from man *himself*. Otherwise man's *selfhood* could again be isolated from his facticity. Human subjectivity is not what it is without being
involved in facticity. If, then, I say that I *myself* execute a
certain action, this excludes that the action is solely the
result of a deterministic influence of facticity, but includes
that this action is not what it is without facticity.

The consequences of this insight are far-reaching.
There is no personal philosophizing without the sedi-
mented philosophies, no personal justice without a legal
order, no personal religiousness without institutions, no
personal love without sensuality, no personal conscience
without biological and sociological infrastructures, etc.
On the other hand, the "I," the origin of the human action,
can never be "produced" by the "pressure" of facticity, for
facticity is not what it is without subjectivity. All "pressure" of facticity *presupposes* the subject and, therefore,
can never *explain* the subject's facticity. Similarly, facticity cannot *explain* the action, for that originates in man's
subjectivity.

The specifically human character, then, of the action
consists in this that the action is always to some extent
done by man *himself*. If I wish to express the meaning of
a certain action, it is not enough to refer to the influence of
facticity: there is also the subject's spontaneity, and
through this spontaneity a meaning is always a new meaning, at least because the subject ratifies or does not ratify

the facticity. The action, then, always co-originates from the subject himself.

"Existence Precedes Essence"

Sartre expresses the acting subject's priority or freedom in his notorious characterization of existentialism: "*Existence* precedes essence." We call his characterization notorious because, for Sartre, his statement is inseparable from atheism. From the fact that man is not a "paper-knife," that is, a thing, and, consequently, not conceived and created by a "superior craftsman," Sartre concludes that man is what he makes of himself. If one abstracts from Sartre's atheism, his statement that *existence* precedes essence can be put to good use: it indicates that we must assign a certain priority to man's subjectivity in all human activity. Man's action is not the result of a deterministic influence exercised by facticity, in the way that a process runs its course under the influence of a unilateral, deterministic cause. Sartre's statement, then, means that man is not a thing like a paper-knife, a stone, a kind of moss or a cauliflower, and his life is not a "process of corruption" (*sic*).

A second reservation must be made with respect to Sartre's statement. A certain priority, we said, should be assigned to the subject: for Sartre this priority is absolute. But the subject as freedom occurs only as involved in a particular situation or facticity, and this means a certain restriction with respect to the leeway of the subject as project. The subject's freedom, then, is not absolute.

"Obvious Decisions"

Because man is a self, it is possible to say that man *himself* acts. The acting of man as a subject is not a process because man executes his action with consciousness of what he does: as a "natural light," man *exists* in the truth, he "stands" in objectivity. The subject as "light" "liberates" the objective meaning of facticity and of the possibilities anchored in this facticity. Man "knows what he is doing."

The fact that man knows what he is doing implies that a decision precedes his acting, that the subject *chooses* among the possibilities left by his facticity. He *decides* to realize this possibility rather than that one. With respect to action on the proper level of his manhood, such a decision or choice is free. For the possibilities implied in the facticity are the subject's *own* possibilities, and it is the subject *himself* who decides to realize this rather than that possibility.

This choice, however, is not absolute, it does not start from "zero." The choice is a decision about possibilities, but possibilities are *real* possibilities only on the basis of a certain facticity. The project which man is is a "thrown project," a choice is a decision about possibilities within a particular situation. On the proper level of being-man, however, there is no situation which *determines* a human action. There is merely question of being appealed to by a particular situation, and it can happen that a certain "decision" then becomes "obvious." The way in which facticity appeals to me co-motivates my decision, but the motive does not have any meaning "in itself": its meaning is co-derived from my subjectivity as project. I *take* the motive as a motive.

My wretchedness, for example, does not drive me into a revolutionary party *just as* a storm drives a ship onto the coast. But my wretchedness appeals to me in a certain way, through which the decision to join the revolutionary party becomes "obvious." The motive, however, is taken by me as a motive, it functions within a particular project, viz., the project to live more prosperously. In function of a different project, e.g., that of resignation, the situation has a different meaning.

Applied to the relationship between free action and passion, this means that man's subjectivity distances itself from every instinctive impulse and breaks its compelling and determining influence. Man's action as a human action, then, is not a being completely fascinated and carried away, as an animal is fascinated by its prey. On the contrary, it is a modifying interference in facticity, by virtue of which the subject distances himself and judges objective reality from a standpoint transcending the here and now appeal.

Note, however, that we are speaking here about human action as *human*. Not every action which can be ascribed to a man is *per se* an authentically human action. We do not claim that passions can never determine man and that an "action" can never be a kind of "discharge" provoked by an instinctive impulse. According to the psychologist Nuttin, however, there are very few ways of behaving which do not contain at least a certain influence or after-effect of insights and considerations which rise above matter. There is at least that specifically human restraint or hesitation through which the instinct is followed with less abandon.

From this standpoint it does not make sense to say that man is "condemned to freedom." On the contrary, one should say that man's *task* is to be man, to act humanly. Thus freedom of action also appears as a task, and in this sense one can say that freedom has to be conquered.

In his choice man, strictly speaking, always faces *several* possibilities, even when there seems to be only one, for he can always choose for or against that possibility. In choosing for or against a particular possibility, man explicitly takes up his involvement in his situation. This involvement means for him both an affective *yes* and equiprimordially an affective *no* to the situation. There is no reality to which man cannot consent to some extent; at the same time, there is no reality to which man can fully and definitively consent. In his choice for or against a particular possibility man explicitly takes up the positive or the negative moment of his involvement in reality, he lets the positive or the negative moment of his *existence* prevail. Freedom of choice explicitly takes up what man, as involved subjectivity, essentially is.

Freedom as "Movement of Transcendence"

When man acts on the proper level of his manhood, he reaches beyond the facticity of his *existence* toward the fulfillment of a possibility that is not yet filled. The new meaning which he thus establishes becomes a new facticity of his *existence*. There is, however, no facticity without potentiality: the newly established meaning opens up another new possibility, for man is a project. Because the acting man continually evokes new possibilities, one can never say that man is "finished." For this reason man may be called a "movement of transcendence" (Merleau-Ponty), a self-transcending movement.

As a self-transcending movement, action is the execution of the project which man is. Because his being is a being-"at"-the-world, it is not possible for man not to execute his own being-a-project. Even if a man decides no longer to realize himself, he still realizes himself—albeit as a lazybone, a good for nothing, a blockhead and an idler. When he decides no longer actively to involve himself in the world, man still builds a world: a world in which broken dams cause thousands of victims, diseases run rampant and nine out of ten children will have to die prematurely. Man cannot do nothing, for doing nothing also is doing something.

5. FREEDOM AS HISTORY

The insight that man, on the proper level of his man-hood, is the execution of the project which he himself is, justifies the use of the term "history" to indicate the special character of the dynamics of human *existence*. To understand this, it is necessary to keep in mind that the dynamics of being-man is entirely different from that of things. Terms such as process, evolution, growth and movement are no longer proper in this context.

The special character of the dynamics of human *existence* has already been sufficiently discussed. At present we are mainly concerned with showing that *existence* as transcendence is "history." Describing man as *existence*, we indicated that it is a being-conscious-in-the-world. We also saw that two levels must be distinguished in *existence:* the level of the ego-body and that of personal consciousness and personal freedom. Obviously, therefore, when *existence* is described as history, this history also must be sought on several levels: we must distinguish at least an infrahuman and a human history. The "history" of the infrahuman, also called "prehistory," leaves room for quasi-processes, but as soon as we reach the level of the properly human, the level of consciousness and freedom, terms such as growth, movement, process and evolution become meaningless.

Nevertheless, it would be wrong to detach human history from infrahuman history, for then we would isolate subjectivity and facticity from each other. Freedom would then no longer be situated, it would no longer be human freedom. Human action, as conscious and free, is framed in a prehistory; conscious and free *existence* is a taking up of a prepersonal history.

The human history of which we are speaking here is

man himself insofar as in his activity, creative of culture, he places himself at a distance from facticity, seizes its objective meaning and realizes the possibilities this meaning contains. For example, in order to provide for his physical needs, man has given rise to a very complex system of economic institutions. This system did not drop out of the sky, but was laboriously built by man. In the past many changes were made in that system, and others will be made in the future. There is "movement," then, in economic life. This "movement," however, is not more or less like the volcanic movements occurring in the earth's crust, nor like the evolution of giant reptiles in the Cretaceous period. The reason is that human subjectivity always plays a role in the economic "movement." It is man who becomes aware of the objective meaning of the system's facticity and who, on the basis of this facticity, projects a more satisfactory system, which he *himself* then brings about. The "matter" with which the economist works is "human matter," and the changes in an economic system are always brought about by the interference of human subjectivity.

The same could be said with respect to language, art, social and religious life, the sciences and philosophy. Without the subjectivity of human *existence* nothing can be understood of the "changes" occurring in the cultural world, and because of this subjectivity these "changes" are not mere processes.

History in the Strict Sense

The temporality of the subject-in-the-world is called history when there is question of man's cultural activity, his pursuits in the political, social, economic, artistic, scientific and religious realms. Moreover, the accepted usage of the term "history" connotes the intersubjective aspect of human action. The history of culture is always a collective history, and the more the world becomes one, the more also history will become the history of all mankind.

In his cultural activity man is rooted in the past, which was constituted by the people who preceded him. Our ancestors tried to humanize the world, and all cultural activity of our time is a taking up of their intentions. In his cultural activity man always distances himself from the constituted, from facticity: he tries to seize its real meaning in order to ratify or reject it, or else modify it. In this way he is continually in dialogue with his fellowmen: the past continues to live in the present and is projected toward a future. Man is never "finished" and his world is never "completed."

6. Freedom, "Liberation" and Work

Any term expressing "human reality" can have a whole spectrum of meanings. Being-a-subject *is*, we said, being-free, but anyone can see at once that, although all men are subjects, they are subjects in different ways. There are "great" subjects, people who are "I"'s in the full sense of the term, "full" personalities, authentic human beings. But there are also people whose subjectivity barely rises above *not*-being-a-subject: their subjectivity lies, as it were, crushed under a heavy burden. Their "I" is only a "small" "I," with hardly any possibilities.

For example, what is the meaning of the subjectivity of an Indian farmer, who has to spend fifteen hours a day in back-breaking labor on a rockstrewn piece of land? Or that of an industrial worker who has found "shelter" in one of Rio de Janeiro's infamous slums? Or that of a neurotic who is torn apart by anxieties and collapses under the weight of his pseudo-religiousness?

To be a subject is to be free, but this can mean all kind

133

of things. Man is distinct from the animal by his subjectivity, but before this *really* means anything, man's freedom must first be "liberated." Man realizes himself, but this *really* means something only when he manages to break away from the burden of a facticity which enslaves his freedom. The history of freedom will never be finished, however, because any form of liberation gives rise to a new form of enslavement. No one can foresee the "direction" which history will take, but we do know where this history began and where, if in a particular place it did not yet begin, it will have to start. The history of freedom's liberation begins with work.

Work as Man's Coming to Be Man

It was Marx who first saw the essential importance of work for man's humanization and for liberating man's "freedom." According to Marx, man realizes himself by turning to nature. He does this through his work. By work nature becomes man's "inorganic body"—a term Marx uses to indicate that there is interaction between man and nature. By his work man dominates nature, liberates himself and becomes authentically human.

The animal also is involved in nature, but in an entirely different way. The animal is fully at one with its activity, it does not distinguish itself from it. The animal's activity stands fully in function of its immediate needs. Man, on the other hand, can distance himself, he makes his own activity the object of his knowing and willing, thereby raising it to a higher level. Unlike man, the animal is a stagnant being. Man begins to distinguish himself from the animal as soon as he begins to *produce*, and the first things he produces are, of course, the necessities of life, his food.

These ideas hold in any form of human society. Work

134

is a process between man and nature, a kind of "metabolism," established, regulated and controlled by man. Through his bodily forces man acts upon nature, but, by changing nature, he also changes himself: he develops the powers and abilities which lie dormant in his own being.

Man, then, is a self-realizing being or—and for Marx this is the same—man is essentially a worker. Work makes man a man. Work, however, becomes really productive only when man begins to make tools; besides, really productive work implies a division of labor: it must be executed as a social task. The product, then, is always a product of common or social labor: work produces society. The division of labor means that people work for one another. Thus work really is a mutual help, as is most evident in modern industrial labor. Man would simply disappear if he did not work. Exactly the same, however, is asserted when one says that man would disappear if people did not work *for one another*. Work, therefore, not only makes man a man but also a fellowman.

Work also constitutes the connecting link in mankind's history. The fact that every generation finds at its disposal the means of work produced by the preceding generations means that every man is permeated with, and dependent upon the past. Man, then, is the origin and the product, the creator and the creature of history, and in this history work occupies the central position. The bond between men is not secured by any "political or religious nonsense," says Marx, but by the continuity of the means of production.

The original and novel point in Marx's description of work is his emphasis on man's self-realization. For Marx work is not purely a means to a goal lying outside work itself, but work is a goal in itself. Man wants to live, to be man; therefore, he wants to work, for working is living, is being-man. For this reason Marx is against work *for wages.* The idea that the laborer must sell his power to work is unbearable to Marx, for in this way work does indeed become a means for an external goal. According to Marx, work is *the* way for man to realize himself, and this is no longer the case when work is wage labor. For the wage laborer life is nothing but a means to live.

While recognizing that the character of a means can never be totally eliminated from work, we think that work should not be reduced to a *mere means.* Even eating and drinking are not mere means to live but also ways of living. Dining is to a certain extent a goal in itself, and the same must be said even more of working. To work *is* to become man.

Modern Work

Although Marx's description of work is original, it is not broad enough to be applicable to work as we know it today. Marx had in mind the kind of labor which in his era drew most attention, viz., the production of material goods. But this kind of work is merely a beginning. As soon as the production of material goods has become so effective that man is able to wrest a surplus from nature, there is room for other modes of self-realization than that contained in work conceived as "production." The pursuit of science and art, sports and games, and many ways of taking care of one's fellowmen become possible only when work, in the narrow sense, has reached a certain level of productivity. "Production," however, always remains a necessary condition for those other ways of self-realization.

As was mentioned, rationality is one of the aspects by virtue of which human activity can be called human. It was Descartes who foresaw what the worker would be able to do if he let himself be guided by the rationality of the physical sciences: man could become "master and possessor of nature." Descartes' dream of the future has become a reality in technology: work has become technical work.

Thus arose the glorification of work as *the* way of man's self-realization and self-humanization and as *the* condition for the establishment of human relations and genuine peace. A labor civilization and a philosophy arose in which work may be called the central reference point.

There is no reason to be surprised by this development. As we saw, work can only be called meaningful for man's *integral* humanity from the moment when he wrests a surplus from nature. Obviously, it was only through technology that this condition was fully satisfied. Moreover, when man really begins to work, he continually has more to do with his fellowmen. Work means man's coming to be man in the intersubjective sense.

Once, however, productive labor has made man's integral self-realization possible, *every* way of human self-realization can be called work. There remains a difference between work and "occupation"—in the sense of busyness—and there remains a difference between work and leisure, but under certain conditions any occupation can be work and any type of work a leisure pursuit. One man's work can be the other's occupation. The truck gardener certainly works, the laborer who cultivates half an acre of homegrown vegetables works and plays at the same time, but the retired gentleman whose enthusiastic hobby is king-sized watermelons can hardly be said to work.

What are the conditions under which any occupation can be called work? What is the *modern* form of labor of which Marx could not yet speak? In our opinion, Kwant offers the best answer to this question. He describes modern work as that human occupation which is performed within the framework of the socially regulated satisfaction of needs and which for this reason implies a social "having to." To work is to be occupied within the framework of providing for needs. These needs are not exclusively bodily needs. Because needs vary in the different phases of history, certain occupations *become* work. Where no need whatsoever is provided for, there no work of any kind is done. At the same time, work implies a social "having to," which, at least in the last instance, is imposed by the needs. The working man undertakes that which, in view of the needs, *has to* be done. This "having to" is socially regulated, either by the official "labor order" or by another form of social collaboration.

Accordingly, work is very one-sidedly described as a wrestling with nature in order to humanize nature. Such a description is hardly appropriate for many contemporary forms of genuine work. Delivering speeches, having conferences, and administering an enterprise are ways of working but not of "wrestling with nature," at least not in the sense which Marx originally attached to this term.

If man's freedom must be liberated before this freedom *really* becomes meaningful, then work evidently is the first step on the road to freedom. Unlike Marx, we do not claim that the economic basis of society *determines* the so-called "higher, spiritual aspects" of man, society and history. Nevertheless, there can be no genuine subjectivity and freedom unless man "goes to work." The West was first to recognize this necessity, it replaced the pre-scientific rationality of work by the rationality of the sciences, that is, it changed work into technology, "invented" management and the legal order and thus liberated freedom. The necessity of work for the humanization of man is so evident that at present underdeveloped countries also realize the need to take over these Western inventions.

As everyone knows, however, today the West criticizes its own inventions in this matter. What does this criticism mean if work is the first and most necessary condition for setting man's freedom free? Did this liberation result again in slavery, albeit of a different kind than the one from which it freed man?

The Slavery of the Technocratic Order

No one can indict technology without making himself ridiculous. Most monuments of genuinely human greatness are unthinkable without technology. To abolish technology would mean anarchy, barbarism, starvation, disease and death—in a word, the loss of everything human which man has managed to conquer in a long and bitter struggle. The rationality man uses in his technical work is a genuinely human good, one of the most eloquent possibilities and expressions of human genius. The power acquired through technology is an affirmation of man's superiority over the mere thing. Technology can never be sufficiently appreciated.

The abundant fruitfulness of physical science and technology, however, is also a danger. It tempts man to make the spirit of technology an absolute, to entrust himself entirely to the perspective opened by science and technology and to expect that they will answer *all* questions and alleviate *all* needs. The attempt to absolutize the *spirit* of technology has given rise to so-called "technocracy." As early as 1933 Marcel pronounced his terrible indictment of it, and subsequently practically all philosophers who still retained any awareness of man's integral reality have sided with him. In a technocratic society the spirit of technology is absolutized. What does this spirit consist of, and what is this absolutism? Two levels must be distinguished here.

On the cognitive level the spirit of technology is determined by the rationality of the sciences. Absolutizing this

139

rationality is called "scientism." In the sciences of nature the world reveals itself insofar as it is calculable and measurable. It is easy to foresee where absolutizing the attitude of physical science must lead, no matter how legitimate this attitude is within physical science itself. The reality of everything which cannot be measured or calculated is simply meaningless for the adherent of scientism, it does not exist for him. To use again the example given before, water is solely H_2O for one who makes science the absolute: all other meanings of water are relegated to the realm of poetry. For the technocrat the Rhine is simply "energy." But why do ordinary people love to take their vacation on the Rhine? One who goes for a swim from a lovely beach most assuredly is not interested in H_2O.

On the affective level also the spirit of technology infects man, manifesting itself in the desire to have and control. We do not intend to deny the positive value of this desire, but what happens when this desire is absolutized? First of all, the possibility of progressively dominating the world tends to asphyxiate man's power to wonder about the world. The more technology dominates, the more man comes face to face with his own creations: he increasingly forgets that the world was already there before he transformed it into energy. The more he "possesses" the world through technology, the less man is capable of gratitude. For gratitude presupposes the reception of a gift, but the world is no longer a gift; it is conquered. In this way pride is fostered.

Secondly, for the technocrat, human beings are not subjects but "bodies," "bodily forces" and "functions" in systems of tools and machines. They are measurable and calculable and treated as such. The technocrat exploits man, even if he pays him a "just wage."

Most victims of technocracy do not realize their condition, at least not through an intellectual reflection upon their way of life. The reality of life, however, can manifest itself also in what Heidegger calls the "mood" of *existence*, its "tonality." It is on the level of this "mood" that the victims of technocracy are conscious of their condition. Not finding oneself at ease in the technocratic order prevails over finding oneself at ease in it. Man does not feel at home in it because his integral being-human, his authentically being-a-person is mutilated. The world of technocracy is exclusively a mathematically calculated world; the rhythm of life becomes more and more the rhythm of a machine, in which man is a "function," his fellowman "another function," and being-together a "coordinate functioning" calculated by the psychotechnician. Technocracy has deprived man of his *selfhood* and reduced him to an anonymous entity, the impersonal "one."

Man, however, cannot behave as an anonymous entity on one level of his life and as a person on a different level. The fact that the depersonalized people of a technocracy do not know what to do with their free time shows this. They have lost their integral selfhood to such an extent that they slavishly follow any form of advertizing or propaganda. Insofar as man profits from technocracy he has also lost his selfhood, for he puts the core of his *being* in *having*, in television sets and motorcars. He loses his selfhood in the products of his technology. From the religious standpoint, the victims of technocracy are among those people who quietly "fade away" from religion because, as they say, they "*get* nothing out of it." The loss of personality has become widespread.

The victim of technocracy is tempted to despair as soon as his blindness disappears: nihilism prevails. Not technology, however, is nihilistic, but technocracy. Technocracy means the *nihil*, the nothing of man's integral personality. Heidegger speaks of "forgetfulness of being" as characteristic of technocracy. Technology is a good but, because man has let himself become fascinated by his own technology, he has not succeeded in mastering his own mastership of the world.

If the technocratic mentality were fully realized, integral human life would be doomed to disappear. But, as we saw, technocracy has become unbearable to man. His protest usually is still only on an affective level, but this affective breach with the system leaves room for asking questions which can be the beginning of a "reversal" (Heidegger).

Camus bears witness to this possibility: "it can happen," he says, "that all of a sudden the whole scenery crumbles. To get up, take the streetcar, work for four hours in the office or factory, take the streetcar, eat, take the streetcar, work for four hours, eat, sleep, all the time in the same rhythm on Monday, Tuesday, Wednesday, Thursday, Friday and Saturday—usually man has no trouble in following this routine. But one day the question 'why' arises. Everything 'begins' in this boredom, once it is colored by wonder. We say 'begins,' for this work is important. Boredom lies at the end of the activities of a mechanized life, but at the same time, it puts consciousness into motion. It arouses consciousness and leads to the consequences. The result is either an unconscious return to the chain or a definitive awakening."

As long as man is still somewhat human, capable of being bored, it remains possible for him explicitly to realize that work—the first step on the road to the liberation of freedom—can thereafter establish new forms of slavery. When he realizes this, then he can no longer escape the question of the meaning of his liberated freedom.

"Bourgeois" Philosophy's Alleged Sense of Doom

The alleged nihilism of technocracy is an abomination for the Marxist, who is a technocrat "by definition." The

142

pessimism of certain Western thinkers about technocracy is for him the last—for the umptieth time—convulsion of the bourgeoisie's sense of doom. Western lamentations over the "mass man" of technocracy merely show that the West is unable to give a *real* answer to the question of what man is. For the Marxist, Western bourgeois philosophy itself now expresses something which is *of necessity* implied in history, viz., the end of bourgeois society.

The Marxist himself has a very simple answer to the question about the meaning of liberated freedom. The liberation of man's freedom through work is at first only to the advantage of the privileged few—those who have seized control of the modern production apparatus. This apparatus, however, is by its very nature social: it can only be operated by many and produce for many, who depend on its products to stay alive. The "fact" that the social means of production are the private property of individuals is for Marx *the* conflict among men: this private ownership *is* absolute power of man over his fellowmen, *is* class struggle, *is* slavery for many, independently of "subjective" intentions. Objective history—the history of work, of course—is on the road to liberate the enslaved freedom of the many. Independently of any "subjective" intentions, the proletariat's "objective" reality moves history toward the moment when *the* conflict will be solved: the moment when the proletariat will take over the means of production. Then man will become authentically human, his freedom will be liberated. When *the* conflict no longer exists, brotherhood and peace will arise, of necessity! Man will become man in both the subjective and the intersubjective sense; the universal labor order will *be* humanity, love, brotherhood and peace. Co-existence in work will be intersubjectivity in the full sense of the term.

Herein lies the great illusion of Marxism. It stands to

143

reason that in and through modern work all men will have bonds with all other men. But every society which assumes social ownership of the means of production will have to appoint certain individuals to manage these means and divide their products. 'There is nothing, however, which can *guarantee* that no new class struggle will then arise. All workers will have bonds with all other workers, but nothing *guarantees* that this bond will be authentic intersubjectivity. A world-wide labor order can be unmitigated hell if the subjects hate one another. Authentic subjectivity requires more than Marx would have us believe.

Suggested Readings

Luijpen, *Existential Phenomenology*, Chapter Three.

Sartre, *Existentialism and Humanism*, London, 1948.

Heidegger, "On the Essence of Truth," *Existence and Being*, London, 1949.

Marcel, *Problematic Man*, New York, 1967.

Karl Marx, *Economic and Philosophical Manuscripts of 1844*, Moscow, 1961.

Henry J. Koren, *Marx and the Authentic Man*, Pittsburgh, 1968.

CHAPTER FOUR

Phenomenology of Intersubjectivity

AM I the only human being? Am I an isolated *existence?* Am I "first" man and do I "next" decide to have or not to have relations with others? These and other similar questions have not yet explicitly been raised. The man I am disclosed himself as a conscious-being-in-the-world, a being which cannot be isolated from the world without losing its manhood. But in my world I encounter human beings. I am the project of my world and make the world a cultural world, but as soon as I encounter another human being in my world, I realize that the other may not be submerged in my project as a worldly thing which receives its meaning from me as creator of culture. What is my relationship with the other?

In order not to interrupt a minimum of systematic presentation, we did not yet discuss the relationship of my *existence* to other *existences.* We must now make this relationship the topic of our discussion. Contemporary philosophy expresses this relationship by saying that *existence* is *co-existence.*

1. To Exist Is to Co-exist

Generally speaking, the term *co-existence* indicates that on no level of his *existence* is man absolutely "alone." The presence of others in my *existence* implies that my being-

145

man *is* a being-through-others. If mentally I remove from my being-man the being-through-others, I would come to the conclusion that I am removing the reality of my manhood itself. Being-through-others, then, is an *essential* characteristic of man. We will develop this idea in the following pages.

Two Objections

Let us first, however, consider two objections against the radically social character of man. No aspect of being-man, we argue, is what it is without the presence in it of other human beings. But, one could object, white blood corpuscles evidently are "aspects" of man; nonetheless, they are not a social reality. A bad answer would be to show, on the basis of biological heredity, that other men also enter the picture with respect to one's blood corpuscles. We call this answer "bad" because it does not speak about man on the level on which man is spoken of as *man*. The same would happen if one were to speak of the human heart as a muscle or a pump. The right answer is that existential phenomenology does not refer to man as an object of biology, but is concerned with man as a *subject;* it speaks of the being-man which *inter alia* is presupposed by the pursuit of biology. This is man as *existent* subject, as project, as "having to be" and its execution, as history. Man is essentially history and, as such, he is radically social.

The second objection is the following. If *existence* is essentially *co-existence*, then the "first man" could not be called "man." We would be willing to accept this consequence, but not without indicating to what extent we find it acceptable. Mankind is estimated to be at least 500,000 years old. What kind of man was that man who lived so long ago? Anthropologists sometimes discover a tribe which, they claim, is 50,000 years behind civilized man. One who studies what the manhood of such primitive people means can even ask himself whether they can really be called men. The question must be answered in the affirmative: they are human beings. But there is also a standpoint from which a negative answer is possible: their manhood has not yet reached authenticity on any level. If we call them human, we do so because these primitives are able to rise to the level of authentic manhood—a possibility which a totem pole or a butterfly does not have. The level of authentic manhood, however, will never be reached if their *existence* does not begin to realize itself as *co-existence* in a much more comprehensive fashion.

Applying these ideas to the objection, the "first man" was not man on an authentically human level because his *existing* was not *co-existing*. Now, the statement that *existence essentially* is *co-existence* applies to man on the authentic level of his manhood. Besides, this is the only level on which there can be question of man. For, if the "first man" is called man because he is able to rise to the level of authenticity, then it is evident that it is only on the basis of authentic humanity that there can be question of such a possibility.

Development of the Idea of Co-existence

In exploring the meaning of *co-existence*, we must keep in mind the distinctions made in the preceding chapters and successively consider the *existent* subject as *cogito* (I think), *volo* (I will) and *ago* (I act); in other words, we must explore the subject in his knowing, willing and acting dimensions.

On the cognitive level the *existent* subject evidently is *co-existence*. This claim applies to the prescientific, the

147

scientific and the philosophical levels. On the prescientific level we find, for example, the perception of a poker. Perceiving a poker is not a question of stimuli reaching my retina. If I hold a poker before a Papuan, there would be just as many stimuli on his retina as on mine, but he would *not* perceive a poker. I am able to perceive a poker because of the way I have seen others behave with respect to a poker: their actions made a certain meaning appear to me. Moreover, other people gave this object a name: they used the term "poker," which sets this object apart from others for me as having a distinct meaning. It is *I* who perceive, of course, but the perceiving *I* only is what it is —perceiving the poker—because the behavior and speech of others are present in my knowing.

The same applies on the level of the positive sciences. The man of science *personally* "sees," but his personal seeing is based on a tradition which is deeply rooted in the remote past. No matter how great a genius the man of science is, if he had to start from a zero level of "seeing," he would not reach any scientific level. The greatest mathematician, for example, depends on the "seeing" of, let us say, an obscure Mesopotamian hunter, who began to mark his spear with notches for every kill he made and thereby discovered the principle of "abstract" numbers. Other people are always present in my personal knowledge on the scientific level.

The same applies also to philosophizing. We saw this in Chapter One, where we called philosophizing a social undertaking *par excellence*. The "classics" of the philosophical tradition *make* us "see." One who today wishes to give a personal expression to reality cannot avoid discussing things that have already been spoken of by others.

On the affective level similar ideas apply. The subject who on this level of his *existence* is involved in the world is characterized by a certain "mood": the "mood" of our time is entirely different from that of people who lived in a primitive world of culture. Between our phase and the primitive phase lies a long history made by other people. By making this history, they also "made" me in my "mood." In my appreciation of values I am a child of the twentieth century, but it was the children of the nineteenth century who made me this.

On the level of action, of subjectivity-as-*ago*, existence also manifestly is *co-existence*. Marx was the first philosopher to put full emphasis on this point. For Marx, the interconnection of history is constituted by *co-existence* in work. The fact that every generation begins with the tools of work produced by the preceding generations means that every man is tied to the past and dependent upon it. Thus, the bond between men is secured by the continuity of the means of production. As we saw, Marx's concept of work is too narrow and this narrow concept plays too large a role in his philosophy. Nevertheless, it remains true that Marx's emphasis on *co-existence* in work has made it possible for modern man to understand the radically social character of the subject-as-*ago*. No man is "alone" in his actions: he always bases himself on meanings established by others.

One could object that all our examples were taken from the world of culture, in which it is a foregone conclusion that other *existences* are involved in the establishment of meanings. But, one could ask, is the same true also for the "natural" world (assuming that this distinction is not meaningless)? Is the "natural" world a system of meanings established by others? And if so, would not the affirmative answer have an entirely different sense?

In reply, let us draw attention to the proper reason why we say that *existence* is *co-existence*, that my being is a being-through-others. This reason is the fact that the others *make* me participate in the world through their

149

behavior and *speech*. Now, even when there is question of the "natural" world, the behavior and speech of the others make me be the thinking, willing and acting subject I am. This is the reason why the other is "present" in my *existence*, why *existence* is *co-existence*. And it is also the reason why the distinction between the cultural world and the "natural" world cannot ultimately be maintained. We do not see an untouched "natural world" in itself with a "virgin eye," because for at least 500,000 years man has already been busy "opening the eyes" of his fellowmen or "throwing dust" into them.

The Social Body of Man

Paying attention to the details of *co-existence*, we could easily lose sight of the totality. Man is "one," he is the unity of a *Gestalt*. The thinking subject, the willing subject and the acting subject are not juxtaposed "elements," but aspects of one and the same reality—man—and it is man who *makes* man *be*. For this reason we must say that "this" man is a New Yorker through New Yorkers, a smoker through smokers, a philosopher through philosophers. Similarly, a sick person is really sick only when he is visited or forgotten; a Negro is a Negro only when Whitey refuses to admit him to his bowling alley or closes the doors of the university to him; a cute little button nose is really a cute little button nose only when others notice it; a baldhead is a real baldhead only when he is called that by others. These examples clearly show the complex *Gestalt* character which our making-one-another-be has. We can distinguish the thinking, willing and acting of the subject, but they cannot be separated from one another or from the totality.

The totality of man which makes man *be* manifests itself even more clearly if we direct our attention to those domains in which man forms groups. This is the realm in which positive sociology is interested. The realization that individual *existence* cannot become authentic unless it embodies itself in forms of *co-existence* is the same as the observation of positive sociologists that the individual man is always found as already incorporated in certain groups, which are strongly determinant in his respect. The positive social sciences empirically detail the philosophical insight that *existence* is *co-existence;* they show how much the others, the group, are present in me when I think that it is *I* who thinks or acts. Every group has "predominant" or accepted views and more or less fixed patterns of acting, "ways of doing things."

Young people are often said to "enter" life, but this is not what happens. Rather, they are "pushed" into it. "Entering" life is in the first instance not much more than being incorporated into the "ways of doing things" that have become the fixed pattern of the group. This incorporation implies that the group makes the individual think, act and be, in accordance with the group's patterns.

Making-one-another-be is the indispensable condition for an authentic, *personal existence.* But, one could say, is not this term "personal" in contradiction with the preceding paragraphs? If what one thinks, does or *is* is the result and repercussion of the group's "pressure," how can making-one-another-be be the indispensable condition for authentic, *personal existence?* Is it still possible to speak of "person" and "subject" if one takes seriously the unmistakable reality that we *make* one another *be?*

Sociologism

Sociologism answer this question in the negative: man is nothing but the product of "social processes." The philosopher should at least once in his life be seriously tempted to adhere to sociologism if he does not wish to minimize the importance of *making*-one-another-be. My many encounters with others leave something behind in my own *existence*. In my dealing with others there occurs a quasi-process of sedimentation, and the quasi-effect of it is called "social facticity" or my "social body." The way I eat, greet others, speak, or think is, at least in the first instance, largely the quasi-effect of the fact that I grew up in the West and not in China. The others influence me, but this "influence" is not a process in the strict sense of the term, not the influence of a thing upon a thing. The reason is that my social facticity remains *my* facticity, it is the facticity of the *existent* subject who I am. As *existent*, the subject is immersed in the social facticity, gives meaning to it and can still do all kinds of things with it. Social facticity, then, is not an effect, not merely the result of unilateral and deterministic causes. The other's "influence" is a *quasi*-process, and the social facticity is a *quasi*-effect.

It is precisely the importance of the subject which is disregarded and ultimately eliminated by sociologism. What man *personally* thinks and does presupposes the social facticity which "deposits" itself in man's *existence* through the others's *making*-him-be. If man does not receive any social facticity from others, he cannot realize himself on any level of authenticity. For example, one who has not learned from others how to think mathematically will never be a mathematician. The fact, however, that man receives his social facticity from others does not mean that his personal thinking and acting are nothing but repercussions of the group's "pressure," for his social facticity itself is not simply the effect of a social process. There is no contradiction between subject and facticity, but these two imply each other.

Accordingly, it is not social facticity "alone" which builds meaning in the thinking and acting of personal *existence*. Insofar as the spontaneity and creativity of the subject transcend social facticity, he can let new meaning appear in the group. The patterns of group life do not have the fixity of a rock.

Analogous ideas apply to the social facticity which lies on the side of the world. Canals and roads, cars and planes, books and libraries, works of arts and museums, schools and hospitals, industrial plants and educational systems—all these and many others belong to the social facticity lying on the side of the world. They form part of man's "inorganic social body." They are the result of a long and common history. The subject has established the world's social facticity; it is also the subject who keeps this facticity alive and projects it toward a new future. History, then, is not a mere process, as Marx thought, but presupposes and implies the human subject, who takes up his social facticity and orientates it in his project of self-realization.

2. The Body as Intermediary

What the world means to the other is certainly accessible to me. The letter I write is for me a matter of pen, paper and an announcement, but for the recipient this same letter may be something he awaits in fear and trembling. *His* fear, however, is accessible to me, has meaning for me. I probably took this meaning into account when I wrote my letter. This means that I took the other *subject* into account: the other is not concealed from me but accessible.

In everyday life such things are accepted as a matter of course. Anyone admits that the patient is accessible to the doctor, the customer to the salesman, the student to the teacher. Some mystery always remains, of course, but this mysteriousness does not imply that I cannot "see" the other as a subject. If philosophers and psychologists have experienced the greatest difficulty in admitting, without qualification, that it is possible for me to see the other subject, the reason for this difficulty must be sought in the fact that Cartesian philosophy had, strictly speaking, made this "impossible."

The Impossibility of "Seeing One Another"

The Cartesian divorce of subject and body makes it impossible to conceive any direct contact between one conscious "I" and another conscious "I": my subjectivity is isolated from my body, which is a machine; my body is isolated from the other's body, which also is a machine; and the other's subjectivity also is isolated from his body. If "we" look at each other, then, this would mean that I "look at a machine" and that you "look at a machine." Thus I cannot really *see* that the other person is sad or happy, I cannot hear that he is furious or frightened to death.

Actually, however, no one admits that he cannot really do this. The philosophers therefore tried to restore this possibility *in spite of* Descartes while maintaining the divorce between subject and body. The usual argument was the argument from analogy.

This argument runs as follows. My interiority manifests itself outwardly in bodily movements of expression: particular inner states, such as joy or anger, are exteriorized by particular bodily movements. Now, I perceive in the others the expressive movements through which I myself exteriorize particular inner states. Therefore, I am

154

justified in concluding that there is an interiority in the others and that in them also there are those inner states which I myself express by means of the bodily movements I now perceive in the others.

Today, however, this argument from analogy is no longer accepted: it does not "explain" the presence of, and the contact with the other as a subject. Aside from the fact that there is not the slightest trace of such an argument in my experience of the other as a subject, the argument also *presupposes* what it wishes to explain, viz., that I am in direct contact with the other as a subject. It speaks of *expressive* movements rather than *mechanical* movements. But, in the Cartesian train of thought, bodily movements are mechanical—the body is a machine—unless one *assumes* that they are movements of a *subject*, who *expresses himself* through them. The existence of a subject "behind" those bodily movements, however, is precisely what the argument had to prove. If I cannot *directly see* the other's subjectivity, then the beings I see laughingly strolling around could still be conceived as machines. Thus the argument from analogy fails to "explain" that I can perceive the others as subjects.

It is not at all necessary, however, to have recourse to such an argument, for the encounter with the other subject is directly and immediately distinguished from that with a mere *thing*. The other's body, at which I look, is not just "a" body, but human, a body subject. It reveals itself directly as not-a-thing. It is the other "in person" whom I see shaking with fear, whom I hear sighing with cares. I feel the cordiality of his handshake, the mildness of his voice, the benevolence of his look. Similarly, one who hates me, despises me, who is indifferent to me, bored by me, who wishes to console, seduce or rebuke me—he, too, is in person present to me. His look, his gesture, his

155

word and his attitude are always *his* look, gesture, word or attitude: he is directly and immediately present to me "in person."

The presence of things reveals itself in an entirely different way. The way a rolling rock comes toward me in a mountain pass is entirely different from the way an angry police officer comes toward me. My desk does not groan under my elbows, my pen does not give me a hurt look when I abuse it; I do not blame the apple which falls on my head; and I do not expect my dog to congratulate me on my birthday.

The other's direct presence to me as another subject is something I simply have to accept as primordially given. Any "proof" is superfluous because this presence is immediately evident.

Is the Body "Intermediary" or Not "Intermediary"?

The assertion that the body "mediates" in interhuman encounters can be misunderstood. Encounters between men are possible because in a certain sense man "is" his body. And insofar as man "is" his body, the encounter with his fellowmen occurs without any intermediary whatsoever. As Marcel has convincingly shown, the categories of "having" do not apply to "my body" without any reservations. The object of "having" exists more or less independently of me; I can dispose of it and do away with it. I "have" a car, a pen and a book. "My body," however, does not exist independently of me, as my pen does; I cannot dispose of "my body" and do away with it, as I dispose of, or do away with my collection of stamps. For "my body" is not "a" body but that which embodies *me*.

If subject and body are not separated from one another, one can understand that in the other's look, gesture, attitude or word I really encounter him as a subject. The other's body is "his body," he lives "in person" in his look, gesture, attitude or word. Thus I encounter the other as a subject when he looks at me with love, hatred or indifference, when he gestures toward me, or addresses words to me, for his body, with its attitudes and movements, is the embodiment of his subjectivity.

Only to the extent that there exists a "certain" non-identity between subject and body can the body be said to "mediate" in the encounter of human beings. There exists such a non-identity; for instance, I cannot fully identify the subject who I am with my feet or my nose. In a certain sense, then, I "have" "my body," for if I were unreservedly "my body," I would be fully encompassed by the world of mere things. My body is the transition from what I *am* without reservation to what I *have* without reservation. I *am* a subject and I *have* a car. But with respect to "my body" neither "being" nor "having" can be affirmed without reservation. "My body" lies "midway" between these two, and to this extent one can say that the body acts as an "intermediary" in the encounter between human beings.

A second reason why the body must be said to "mediate" in my encounter with others lies in this that the other's body also makes it possible for me to enter into his world, the complex of meanings existing for him. Through his body, this complex of meanings for him becomes also a complex of meanings for me. When, for example, I sit alongside the driver, I enter by "way" of his body and its extension—the car—into the meaning which the road, hills, curves, narrow bridge and oncoming traffic have for him. If I am nervous because of his excessive speed, he enters by "way" of my body into the meaning which the narrow bridge we are approaching has for me. Similarly, the words my friend uses to describe distant lands I have never seen place me into his world. Through

157

his words I enter into his world and his world becomes
meaningful to me: his world becomes my world, our
world.

To Co-exist as to "Accompany"

All this indicates that the other is present to me in a
very special way. My encounter with him reveals to me
that he is "not a thing" but *existence*, an origin of meaning. He "accompanies" me, he is my "companion," which
a thing cannot be, and for this reason I can speak of "we."
But, is it right to say so explicitly that the other accompanies *me*, is *my* companion? Am I not *his* companion? By
what right would I "first" affirm myself and only "next"
the others as the mass above which I elevate myself? No,
the others are like me, I do not distinguish myself from
them: they are those among whom I *also* am: *we* accompany one another, we are fellows.

In the following pages we will use the term "to accompany" in reference to *co-existence* as encounter with, and
presence to the other as a subject. In the preceding section
these same terms did not receive the emphasis we have in
mind here, because they referred there to the being-
through-others which gives me my social facticity in a
quasi-processlike way. Here, however, "encounter" and
"presence" lie on a more personal level: they refer to a
person-to-person relationship in the stricter sense of the
term. Before discussing the various forms of being each
other's companion, we wish to emphasize that the terms
"encounter" and "presence," previously used to indicate
the reciprocal implication of subject and world, are used
here in an entirely different sense, for the other whom I
encounter reveals himself as a meaning which is distinct
from that of a thing. His presence reveals him as one
"like-me-in-the-world," a meaning which I never notice

when I encounter a thing. That is why he is my "companion-in-the-world." Similarly, the term "dialogue" differs radically here from the dialogue I have with worldly things. Unlike the thing, the other subject answers my questions as another "I," he answers me as I answer him when he asks a question.

Modes of "Accompanying One Another"

Positive sociology describes the manifold forms of accompanying one another and attempts to formulate the empirical laws governing the interaction within those forms of being a "we." This task will obviously never be finished, for man's way of behaving toward his fellowmen are infinitely varied. The relationship of "I" and "you" varies, for instance, when there is question of working together, drinking together, travelling together and having an accident together. Likewise, the "we" of a labor union differs from that of a military barrack or a convent, the "we" of a hospital ward is not the same as that of a youth hostel or a hockey club.

It is essential to realize that the pluriformity of being-companions lies on different levels. People speak of "human relations" in the family, the school, factory, or office, in the armed forces, medical assistance, spiritual care, etc. Describing these relations and formulating the "rules of the game" governing the fundamental forms of man's dealing with his fellowmen is the work of the sociologist. One can also observe, however, that in the many changes which have occurred in human relationship "genuine humanity" has been lost. Such a remark is no longer concerned with sociological forms of being-companions but is interested in the conditions which permit us to call human relations "human" in the full sense of the term.

All this indicates that there is every reason for making

a distinction between *sociological* forms of companionship and others, which we will from now on call *ethical*. In any sociological form man can be authentically human, less human or even inhuman. This remark obviously implies that man *is* not in the same way as an ashtray or a cauliflower *is:* the being of man is a "having to be," it has a certain destiny.

The sociologist and the ethicist investigate the character of the many forms which human fellowship can have with different intentions. Both describe fundamental forms corresponding to their intention or attitude. We will limit ourselves here to the fundamental ethical forms, which are hatred, indifference, love and justice.

First, however, we wish to observe that it is not possible to speak true to life about love and justice if these terms are taken to refer to *commandments*, at least not if *commandments* are understood as laws imposed upon man from without. For then one can never show that man *ought* to love and be just, in the sense of an inner *ought*, i.e., that love and justice are demands flowing from man's own being. Hatred and indifference also are modes of being-man, but modes in which man *ought not* to realize himself. Note also that hatred, indifference, love and justice are not juxtaposed as things, but modes in which the one, concrete man realizes himself. One can even say that all four are present in concrete man, but that the accent falls on one of them.

3. HATRED

For the phenomenology of hatred we can base ourselves fully on Sartre's explicitation of the "look." While a look is not *per se* a look or stare of hatred, what Sartre says about *the* look appears applicable only to the look of hatred. For Sartre, as for all phenomenologists, the existence of the other as the other is immediately evident. This general position, however, receives a wholly unexpected turn when Sartre investigates the situation in which the existence of the other as the other becomes accessible to me. It is only disclosed to me, he holds, when the other looks at me. The other subject always reveals himself as "one who looks at me" and never as anything else.

What the Look Is Not

Catching the other's look is not perceiving a quality—"looking"—among other qualities, such as blue, beautiful or cross-eyed, of an eye or of any object functioning as an eye. Sartre speaks of an object "functioning" as an eye because the look reveals itself not only in the convergence of the pupils but also in the snapping of twigs—e.g., during an assault in the dark—in the sound of footsteps, followed by silence, in the half-open position of shutters or the slight movement of a curtain. All these objects "function" as an eye. To catch the look of someone, Sartre says, is not perceiving his eyes or certain qualities of his eyes, it is not perceiving an object-in-the-world, but to become conscious that I am being *looked at*.

To Be Looked at

What does it mean that I am being looked at? Sartre's example clearly illustrate the exclusive meaning which the look has for him. Imagine, he says, that, driven by jealousy, I look through the key hole of a room in order to catch the occupant in a compromising situation. In doing this, I am fully with the "object" of my looking and with the door or the key hole, which for me have the meaning of being obstacle or instrument of my actions. Suddenly I hear footsteps in the corridor, followed by silence: someone else is looking at me! At the very moment I realize that I am being looked at, I experience that I am an object for the other.

My experience of being looked at by the other discloses to me the meaning of the other's subjectivity: under his stare I am as a thing in his world, I experience the death of my own subjectivity. As a "living" subject, I am the co-source of the system of meanings which the world is for me: when I look through the key hole, the walls, the door, the lock, the key hole and the semidarkness of the corridor derive their meanings as obstacles or instruments from my subjectivity; they function at the service of my intentions. As a "living" subject, I am a self-project, I am not what I am, but am what I am not. I am master of the situation and hold my possibilities in my own hands. As a "living" subject, I am also the execution of my self-project, I am the spontaneous co-source of ever new meaning. All this, however, changes when the other's subjectivity appears on the scene.

First of all, the other deprives me of my subjectivity as co-source of meaning. I no longer control the meanings of the door, the walls, the darkness of the corridor: they now relate to the other's subjectivity and have ceased to function at the service of my intentions.

Next, the other's stare means the death of my potential being as a subject. I could try to hide in a dark corner, but the other controls that possibility by his own power to dispel that darkness with his flashlight. My possibility to hide becomes his possibility to unmask and identify me. Every action I execute can become, under his stare, an instrument serving him against me. Under his stare I am no longer master of the situation and I no longer hold my possibilities in my own hands.

Finally, under the other's stare my freedom as transcendence is immobilized. I have to consider myself a slave, for I depend on a freedom which is not mine.

The feeling of shame I experience summarizes what I am in the other's eyes. Looked at by him, I am ashamed. Shame is the recognition that I am the object the other stares at and judges. He merely has to look at me and, at once, I am what I am. For the other I *am bent* over the key hole just as a tree *is bent* by the wind; I *am* for him *indiscreet* just as a table *is round* or a cauliflower *is rotten:* for him I *am* a thing in the midst of things. I am for him what I am.

In a single sentence Sartre generalizes his view of the meaning which the other's subjectivity has: if there exists even a single other person, then the very fact that his subjectivity arises before me makes me be an object. Alluding to the Christian notion of original sin, he says: "My original fall is the existence of the other." Thus I am always in danger, and this danger is not an unfortunate circumstance but the permanent structure of my being-for-the-other.

It may be useful to point out that Sartre does not wish us to understand the destruction of my subjectivity-as-freedom and my reduction to a thing in the most literal sense: I am fully *conscious*—which a thing is not—of the fact that in the other's eyes I am a "thing." Thus I cannot say that I am not a subject. There is no longer question, however, of the "fullness" of authentic subjectivity. Under the other's stare my freedom degenerates into an "attribute" of the "thing" I am for the other. I am "for myself" what I am for the other, but I have no control over what I am for the other when he looks at me. My freedom, then, no longer has any *real* or authentic content.

Hatred

The look of which Sartre speaks is a very special kind of look, but he absolutizes and generalizes its meaning without the slightest sign of reserve. Sartre's look is the hateful stare, which does not accept me as a subject, which does not tolerate that I as a subject project my own world, but which throws me down as a thing among the things of the world by murdering my possibilities. What Sartre says about the look does express something real: it is an ingenious description of the hateful look, and that look is a reality. We do not have the slightest intention of denying this reality.

At the same time, we have no intention of admitting that Sartre correctly describes *the* look, that is, that man can only look at his fellowmen with hatred. There is also a benevolent look, a merciful and forgiving look, an understanding, exhorting, encouraging look—in a word, a loving look. Sartre does not mislead us by what he says but by implying that there cannot be anything else but what he expresses in his analysis.

A question that could come to mind is the following. Suppose that I am mistaken when, bent over the key hole, I think that I hear footsteps? Even then, Sartre argues, I do not err in my certainty of being looked at. The other's look is so real that I abandon my plan or, if I persevere in it, I can hear my heart beat and I sharpen my ears to the slightest sound, the slightest creaking of the stairs. I am not mistaken about the other's presence. The other is everywhere, under me, above me, in the neighboring rooms, in a dark corner of the corridor. Only the empirically verifiable "being there," the concrete, historical event which we express by saying: "There is somebody approaching," remains doubtful, bnt not his presence. I can be mistaken about the object revealing the other's presence, but I am not mistaken in my certainty that I am being looked at by him.

"And in This Way I Recover Myself"

There is only one way for me to regain my subjectivity, frozen by the other's stare. I am an object for the subject who the other is, but I am never an object for an object. To liberate myself from my state of being-an-object, I will rise and try to reduce the other to an object by my stare. "And in this way I recover myself."

All concrete human relations, then, are, in principle, settled for Sartre: either the other reduces me to a thing in his world or I keep his subjectivity under my control by making it an object for me. There are no other possibilities. A subject-to-subject relationship is not conceivable. The essence of interhuman relationship, therefore, is not "being with" but conflict. So-called love is "essentially a fraud," and any will to be loved is a will to possess the other's freedom. Respect for the other's freedom is an idle word.

The "Us"-object and the "We"-subject

According to Sartre, the great complexity of human relations does not modify the fact that the essence of these relations is conflict. He recognizes the reality of the "us"-experience, but describes it also in terms of being looked at. In the "us"-experience there is a third who looks at "us." My relation with the other is nothing but "conflict," but when a third looks at "us," I experience not only my own self-estrangement but also that of the other: we occur in the world of the third as a thing, he holds "us" in his power. In the absence of a third, I fight with the other, but under the stare of a third I experience that "we" are fighting. We are ashamed because a third looks at "us."

Certain situations reveal the "us"-object very clearly. The class consciousness and solidarity of oppressed workers in reference to their oppressors is nothing but the experience of being stared at by a third, the ruling class. Under the ruling class's look, "we" live in estrangement. The Jews also are united, but only under the eye of the

165

anti-Semite. If the term "love" has any meaning, it could be used for these modes of solidarity: "To love is to hate the same enemy."

The "us"-experience, then, is merely a more complex form of being looked at and, as such, leaves only one possibility of liberation: the oppressed class will rise and with its own stare reduce the oppressing class to a "them"-object.

Sartre realizes that there exists also a "we"-subject, which is revealed to us through our common goals and instruments. "We" use a highway and a gas pump; "we" oppress the workers, "we" destroy our oppressors. There is question here of a certain solidarity between subjects. But for Sartre, this "we" is a purely subjective experience of an individual consciousness, only the way in which "I" experience myself among others, only an ethereal symbol of an absolute solidarity between subjects which cannot be realized.

Death

From the standpoint of my self-realizing subjectivity, death is absurd: it "simply" puts an end to my self-realization. My ability-to-be solidifies into the compact density of the thing. Death deprives my life of all meaning. My death, however, has meaning for the other. In my death he definitively triumphs over me: I am no longer able to stare back at him but become a helpless prey of his stare. I now am what I *am*, a thing—just as the other has always considered me. To understand the meaning of my future death, I must conceive myself as the future prey of the other. As long as I am alive, the other will try to murder my subjectivity, but it is only in death that he defininitively triumphs over me.

Retrospect

Sartre's fascinating description of the look in his work BEING AND NOTHINGNESS undoubtedly is a splendid analysis of a degenerate society, but his readers will refuse to accept that even in today's "rotten world" there exists nothing but hatred which cannot bear that the other is a subject realizing himself in the world and which, therefore, cannot rest until the other is definitively reduced to a thing. Sartre reduces the many forms which the "we" can assume to a single pattern: the conflict between the hateful look and the hated being looked at. He leaves no room for any genuine *co-existence*, for intersubjectivity in the sense of being-subjects-together. The only possible reply to such a position is: "There are more things in heaven and earth than are dreamt of in your philosophy."

Let us add that we are not concerned here with Sartre the man, but only with the philosophy he presents to us in BEING AND NOTHINGNESS. His life and involvement in affairs for human freedom show loving concern for fellowmen, but we have to take his philosophy as he presents it. Taken as such, it does not appear to leave room for an interpretation which would say that Sartre "really" wished to depict the true meaning of inauthenticity in man's dealing with his fellowmen. As it stands in his book, his philosophy is a philosophy of hatred.

4. INDIFFERENCE

Even when I hatefully look at the other and "see" nothing in him but a thing, I am still conscious of the fact that he is a subject and I encounter him "in person." What Sartre says of the look explicitates only the *answer*

167

man gives to his consciousness of the other's subjectivity, and this answer, according to Sartre, can only be hatred.

Hatred means that I cannot accept that my fellowman is a subject, cannot bear that he realizes himself as a person, brings about his own personal history. Hatred means that I refuse to dwell "together" in "our" world and bring about "our" history. Hatred is an attempt to reduce the other subject to a factor in my project of the world, to integrate him into the system of meanings I project for myself. Doing that is slavery and murder. He who hates his brother is a murderer, for he destroys the subjectivity by which his brother is a human being.

As was mentioned, being-companions or fellows has more variations than Sartre would have us believe. There is also love, which is exactly the opposite of hatred. In "between" these two, however, lies a way of relating to fellowmen which perhaps occurs most frequently, viz., the way of indifference. We must now discuss this attitude.

The "We" of Indifference

I am indifferent with respect to most people. When I encounter them in my world, I recognize at once that they are subjects. I address them as "you," for I realize that I am dealing with another "I," one "like me" in the world, one who "accompanies" me and with whom I am "together" in the world.

Generally speaking, the terms "encounter," "accompany," "you," "together" and "we" imply that the human being I encounter differs from the things in my world. I never call a thing "you"; I realize that I can never receive a personal answer from a thing and for this reason I do not address a thing as a person, a "you." Similarly, things do not "accompany" me and I am not "together" with things. All these terms, however, become increasingly more meaningful as human relations become more meaningful, more authentically human.

We submit, however, that the "we" which occurs most frequently is the "we" of indifference, the dull, empty and unfeeling "we" of a society which is increasingly losing its humanity. Let us start with an example. What meaning does the man behind the ticket counter have for most travellers? Most people just snap: "Chicago, round trip coach," and put some dollars on the revolving disk. A few seconds later, the ticket appears on the same disk, together with their change. What does the man behind the counter mean to most people? His meaning is the function which he fulfills, and for him the people he encounters in his function are identical with the label "traveller."

How many human beings does the ticket clerk "encounter" during his eight hour shift? One can say 756, but also two—the two who addressed him in an "entirely different way": the boy who said: "Chicago, coach, round trip, please," and the girl who flashed a smile while saying: "Chicago, round trip, coach." All the others demonstrated the "we" of indifference. In their "encounter" with the clerk there was a "we"-consciousness, which is not the case when I take my ticket from an automatic dispenser. The "you" contained in the "we" of indifference has no other meaning than that of a quality: one quality or function—traveller—meets another quality—ticket clerk. Our whole contact is limited to the meeting of those functions. The other does not concern me and I do not care who stands behind the counter: he is for me simply a ticket clerk. If someone else were to take his place, I would not care, just as the ticket clerk remains indifferent as to who snaps: "Chicago, round trip, coach." The "we" of our contact is the "we" of indifference.

The "He"

This kind of "you" can be appropriately expressed by the term "he" (or "she"). For the experience of the "he, there before the class," the "he, there on the operating table," or the "he, there behind the desk" can be fully expressed in a series of predicates expressing the qualities ascribed to "him" in an objective judgment: "he" is ill, "he" is a book keeper, "he" is sensuous, authoritarian, learned, a publisher, handsome, Jewish, etc. The experience of the "he" is like that of a "filled out questionnaire," a "file card" (Marcel). Exactly the same happens when our relations, as described above, are "mutual": "he" is a teacher and "I" am a student; "he" is a doctor and "I" am ill; "he" is a Jew and "I" am a Christian. In other words, "he" is a file card and "I" am a file card; "we" are filled out questionnaires.

It is not difficult to recognize in this "we" the "we" of bureaucracy, administration and a world ruled by technocracy. It is the "we" of indifference, in which no one is someone because no one cares for anyone. But "seeing" in the other nothing but a "he" is a reality, a way people treat each other that is just as real as Sartre's hateful stare. However, is it the only possible way I can meet my fellowman? Obviously not.

An Objection

Are we not going too far here by speaking about indifference in connection with simple functional encounters? The term "indifference" refers to a relationship which is not what it ought to be. But, ought the encounter of traveller and ticket clerk to be more than the meeting of two functions? What ought a waiter to be more than a waiter? Can one expect a quarterback to be more than a quarterback? In summary, can one reproach functional relations for being functional? Why, then, the pejorative label of "indifference"?

Obviously, we do not wish to suggest that functionality is something that ought not to exist in society. One who eliminates all functional encounters would eliminate all humanity embodied in our society. We do not use the term "indifference" because relations are functional, but only because, and to the extent that, they are *purely* functional. In a purely functional relationship there is *no trace whatsoever* of affectivity. It stands to reason, of course, that not every functional encounter can be permeated with the highest degree of love. Yet, every functional encounter ought to participate in a *general* affective attitude toward man, which would make it cease *at once* to purely functional. There is no need for an explicit act of love, but there ought to be a general loving disposition. The latter is practically beyond definition, but its presence in inter-human relationships is experienced as beneficial and its absence is felt as something painful. This absence is rightly called "indifference." Something is lacking which ought to be there: I experience myself as "alone" and the other as "far away."

Am I not more than the sum total of my qualities? Not more than the object of an "objective" judgment? What does it mean that I am "alone" when the other is "far" from me? The fact that I "miss" the other, that I can "miss" him, points to a more original call, the call to togetherness.

Encounter

In the authentically human sense the term "encounter" is loaded with an affectivity of which there is no trace in

171

the indifferent "we," it shows a kind of participation in the personal life of the other as one for whom I "care." This is precisely what is lacking in the encounter of indifference, in which certain qualities "bump" into each other. But there are human encounters in which I obviously experience much more than that. The following example is borrowed, with some modifications, from Marcel.

I am standing in a car of the Paris subway. The car is filled to overflowing and, whenever the train lurches, I "bump" into one of my fellow travellers. Nobody pays any attention to this: we are for one another "travellers in a full subway car." On the platform of the St.-Michel station, from which another train has just departed, only one man is waiting. He opens the door and "bumps" into me. It is possible that he will just "bump" into me, but also that something entirely different will happen. A certain feeling may grow between us, if only because of the trouble I take to make room for him, the friendly smile on his face, or the tone of his voice when he says "I am sorry" while his foot lands on my toes. What is that between this man and me, that reality between us, which both of us feel when we get out and go our separate ways? It is almost nothing, but during the short trip it exercised a hidden kind of "causality" in such an effective way that, if the next day I happen to meet the same man again in the Louvre, I would be inclined to speak to him and say: "Hey, are you too here?"

My encounter with this man becomes unintelligible if one were to say that I "bumped" into him as I bump into a closed door. The term "encounter" now expresses a reality, a "we" with a more profound meaning, permeated with genuine affectivity and humanity. That man was one for whom I "cared"; I did not wish him to miss the train despite the lack of room. And he also "cared" for me, as was evident from the tone of his voice when he gingerly stepped on my toes.

The most striking aspect of our situation, however, is that the objective qualities, which could have been said of both of us, remained wholly in the background during our encounter. Only now I realize that this man was rather stout and that there was something wrong with his left eye. But I did not reduce him to the predicates "fat" and "cross-eyed." If I had done this, what happened between us would never have become a reality and, on seeing him again the next day in the Louvre, I would not have spoken to him, but simply have said to myself: "There is that cross-eyed fatso again."

5. LOVE

Like hatred and indifference, love is a mode of being-companions, of *co-existing* in mutual presence as subjects. The example given at the end of the preceding section could serve as a starting point toward understanding what love really means. One can readily see in that example a first beginning of what may be called authentic love. Let us see what this love implies.

Subjectivity as Appeal

The loving encounter always implies the other's appeal to my subjectivity. A call goes out from him, embodied in a word, gesture, look or request. These signify an invitation addressed to me, the true meaning of which cannot easily be expressed in words. The other's appeal, however, always invites me to break with my self-centeredness, my fascination with my own concerns.

The compulsive way in which I can be centered on

myself and my interests may make it very difficult for me to understand the other's appeal to me. To *see* a certain reality, I need more than eyes; to understand the meaning of the other's appeal, I need a certain attitude in which I have already broken away to some extent from pre-occupation with myself. One who is wholly permeated with pride or greed "sees" nothing, for the other's appeal is not brutal, not bent on conquest, it always leaves room for a refusal. It does not present itself as a demand, and for this reason it is possible for me not to see the other's appeal. If I am fully absorbed by my own interests, I will not understand the other's appeal. Fully pre-occupied with myself, I am *a priori* convinced that I am "excused from everything," so that I am insensitive to any appeal.

In daily life I am used to playing a role: I am a physician, a teacher, a judge, minister or laborer. As a judge I face the delinquent, as a teacher, the student, as a physician, the patient, as a minister, the seeker or sinner. But who are they, those delinquents, students, patients, seekers and sinners? They are the people who appeal to me, but I will not understand their appeal if I identify myself with the role I play. For such an identification means that I am pre-occupied with myself, so that I close myself to the other's *real* appeal to me.

What the Appeal Is Not

First of all, the other's appeal may not be understood as the attractiveness of his or her bodily or spiritual qualities. Otherwise love would be impossible if the other does not have attractive qualities and it would have to cease when those qualities are lost. Qualities can at most give rise to an enamoredness, a desire to "be near the other," but is love not much more? Qualities are listed on a "file card," but I do not really love a "file card." If my friend suffers the loss of his beloved, I cannot console him by obtaining from a computer a file card listing her qualities, finding a woman having the same qualities and introducing her to my friend with the words: "No need to mourn any longer, here is your beloved."

Similarly, the other's appeal to me may not be identified with any explicit request. A request expresses a need based on the other's factical situation, on what he "already" is. Even if I materially satisfy that request, the other can go away very much dissatisfied. He may realize that "my heart is not in it" when I give him what he asks, that he disturbs me, that I am distracted or absentminded. I satisfy his request, yet he is dissatisfied. The reason is that his appeal to me is more than an explicit request for something: he does not merely "make" a request, he "is" an appeal.

"Be With Me"

The other's appeal to me relates to what he is over and above his facticity, viz., a subject. His subjectivity *itself* is the appeal addressed to me, an appeal to share in his subjectivity. Marcel expresses this appeal in the words: "Be with me." The other appeals to me to give up my self-centeredness, to share in his subjectivity, accept, support and increase it.

A New Dimension of Existence

To understand the appeal "Be with me," we said, I must already have overcome to some extent my fascination with myself. On the other hand, it is precisely the other's appeal to me that enables me to liberate me from myself. His appeal reveals to me an entirely new, perhaps wholly unsuspected, dimension of my *existence*. Who am

175

I? Am I not more than the sum total of my objective qualities, more than a file-card, more than the role I play? I am, indeed, more than my facticity because I am a subject and, therefore, freedom. As freedom, I transcend every form of facticity and I continually extend myself toward a never-finished future, in order to establish myself always more securely in my world. But, now the other's appeal to me makes me see that I am not called to realize myself in the world as an egoist, it makes me see that I am called to realize myself in the world *for the other*. His appeal calls me to "conversion," to a change in my self-realization, I "see" that I must conquer the world in order that *the other* can *exist*.

Love as "Yes" to the Other

The other's appeal and my consciousness of my own destiny demand that I give an answer, an answer adapted to the appeal "Be with me." A piece of information, a crust of bread, a coin *are* not the answer sought of me. On the contrary, I realize that they can be means by which I could cheaply escape the answer which I really owe the other. His "*Be* with me" is an appeal to my *being;* giving him bread or money can mean that I reply: "Be satisfied if I give you from what I *have*." Thus I would again lock myself up in my own world, in the hope that the other will never again disturb me. I remain alone, and the other remains far away.

Because the other's appeal does not come from his facticity, the appropriate response also does not primarily refer to his facticity. This is the reason why my destiny for the other is so hard to define. The appeal *is* not an explicit request, the response is not the material granting of a desire but a response to his subjectivity. As an embodied subject, the other is the source of meaning: he continually and freely gives meaning to his facticity and his world. His appeal to me means that he invites me to affirm him as a subject, offer him a possibility to *exist*, consent to his freedom, accept, support and share his freedom. My "yes" to his appeal is called "love."

There is little danger that the term "love" will be misunderstood here as an insipid kind of sentimentality or lax permissiveness. Sentimentality does not *act*, does not accomplish anything in the world. One who joins others in singing "We shall overcome" and cries with emotion on the way home, has not yet made the world more human, has not yet really loved anyone. Love is the "yes" to the other's subjectivity, a subjectivity that is immersed in the body and involved in the world. One who loves his fellowman takes care of the other's body, builds hospitals, constructs roads, tames rivers, blocks the sea, establishes traffic laws, opens schools and prisons, humanizes the economic, social and political structures of society, etc. He does all this in order that it may be possible for the other to be a subject, a self free.

Similarly, love is not permissiveness, acquiescence in the other's capricious desires. To affirm, will and support the other's freedom is not the same as indulging his capriciousness, for the other's *real* freedom is also a being bound to the truth of his own essence and the true destiny of his being. Let us call this destiny "happiness," without making any attempt here to say in what this happiness consists. It could be material possessions, power, wisdom, virtue, sexuality, perhaps even the "possession" of God. No matter what my conviction is about what human happiness is, this conviction obviously will give an orientation to my love for the other. In executing my "yes" to the other's subjectivity, it is not possible for me not to have any opinion or intention about the destiny of freedom. In the same way I cannot be indifferent to what the other,

177

whose selfhood I affirm, thinks about this destiny. If, for example, he thinks that this destiny is to subjugate all men to the tyranny of one, then my love for him and for all obliges me to oppose him and to close, if necessary by force, the roads that would lead him to his "destiny."

How simple it is to write this! But we are actually touching here again a mystery: the absolute good is impossible. There exist "absolute barbarians," people who are always ready to sacrifice others to their caprices and lust. Our "yes" to their subjectivity may and must assume the form of resistance. Love sometimes must make victims, and he who does not accept this simply makes "other victims." Man's recognition of man excludes intolerance and tyranny, but there must be no tolerance of intolerance.

Appeal to the Beloved

In my love of the other I am also concerned with myself. Note that we are still dealing here with love as active turning to the other, not with the desire *to be loved* in return. But even in love as active turning to the other, my love is in a certain sense also concerned with myself. The reason is that, by willing the other's freedom, love is in a certain sense defenseless. It displays infinite trust, and by this very fact surrenders itself to the other. But this very trust and its defenselessness themselves are an appeal of the lover to the beloved. Love, then, is also concerned with the lover himself.

Let us first see what this self-interest is *not*. Love's appeal to the beloved is not the will to draw advantage from one's affection for the other. If I love the boss's daughter in order to promote my career, I do not really love her. Similarly, a nurse who "lovingly" takes care of the sick in order to become head nurse or to "gain an eternal crown in heaven" for herself does not really love her patients.

Secondly, love's appeal to the beloved does not mean that the lover wishes to force, dominate or possess the other. Love wills the other's freedom, it does not wish to reduce him or her to a puppet, but desires that the other in person freely chooses what is in keeping with man's destiny.

The third aspect of self-denial contained in love is a little more difficult to grasp. In love I destine myself for the other, but I realize that, in doing this, I also go forward to my own destiny, the fulfillment of my own being. I see that my proper self is the available self. Being available to the other offers me a possibility to fulfill my own manhood. Thus one can ask: may I make this self-fulfillment, to be found in destining myself for the other, the *motive* of my love? Let us put it more concretely. What conclusion could the other draw if I were to say that I love him or her only because there is no other way in which I can find self-fulfillment? Obviously, the other would conclude that I do not really love him but only myself. While love, then, *actually* is also in my own interest, this interest cannot be the motive of my love.

Positively considered, love's appeal to the beloved can only be understood when one sees that willing the other as a free subject cannot be fruitful unless the other ratifies this will by his own "yes." Love does not wish to force and thus is, in a certain sense, defenseless. But the lover *cannot will* that his love be not understood, not accepted, not fruitful. That's why love is also an appeal to the beloved, an appeal which we would like to explicitate in the words: "Accept that I be at your disposal." Even if love is obliged to close certain roads to the beloved, it cannot do otherwise than will that the beloved *himself* avoid these roads. Love cannot be satisfied with making it materially

179

impossible for the other to go certain roads: it refuses to force the other. Love's appeal to the beloved, then, means a prayer to the beloved that he *himself* see that this road and not that one will lead him to his destiny.

The Creativity of Love

All the lines of love converge in one point: the "you." It is always the "you" that is at stake in love, and wherever the "you" is not at stake, love loses its authenticity or is even wholly destroyed. Pithily expressed, the motive of my love is "you." I love you because you are you. I love you because you are lovable, but you are lovable because you are you.

This *you* does not have here the neutral sense of "another I," it is not the "he" encountered in indifference, and even less the hateful other who wishes to murder my subjectivity. The "you" of whom there is question here is the "you for whom I care." This expression, however, is almost meaningless if the reality to which it refers is not alive in me, if I have no experience of what it means to love.

Science and its special type of experience tells me nothing about the "you for whom I care." The reality of this "you" is not disclosed by an objectivistic psychology, which produces a "file card" listing qualities or describing character, temperament, aptitudes and deviations. Obviously, we do not mean that love can no longer see that the other is stupid, immature or uncouth. Love, however, refuses to reduce the other to a series of predicates, and it is precisely love which makes the lover clearly see what the other is over and above his qualities.

All this merely establishes a fact. After the preceding reflections, however, due weight can be given to this fact and help us to penetrate more deeply into the true character of love, understood as an *active* turning to the other. We would like to conceive this activity as creativity.

In which sense can the subject be called active or creative? As a *knower*, the subject is, as we saw, rather limited in his activity: the knower must *let* reality be what it is. For this reason to know is not a creative activity. The subject's *being-"at"-the world*, however, may rightly be called creative. In doing carpentry work or engaging in artistic pursuits, I do not merely *let* reality be: I "make" it be, I build a new meaning.

We would like to ascribe to love also a kind of "making be," the building of a *new* meaning. But this *making-be* differs from the mutual *making-be* described when we pointed out that *existence* is *co-existence*. We then stated that a sick person is sick only when he is visited or forgotten, that a cute little button nose is a cute little button nose only when her boyfriend notices it, that a baldhead is a baldhead only when others ridicule him, and that a Jew is a Jew only because of the pressure of anti-Semitism.

The risk of misunderstanding present in these examples cannot easily be avoided. One could say, for instance, that a Jew is a Jew even when there are no anti-Semites, that a sick person is sick even when he is not visited or forgotten, and that a baldhead is bald even when he is not the butt of jokes. But such an objection assumes that being a Jew is a purely biological matter, that a sick person is sick just as a cauliflower is rotten, and that the baldhead is bald just as a billiard ball is smooth. Such a view disregards the *human* aspect of being a Jew, sick or bald. A baldhead is not bald as a billiard ball is smooth because the baldhead as a subject is related to his bald pate, he gives meaning to it, and the kind of meaning he

181

gives to it depends largely on the way others treat him. That's why we say that a baldhead is a baldhead only when others ridicule him.

The essential point of the preceding examples is this. In my encounter with the other I am the bearer of a being-for-the-other which is, at the same time, a being-through-the-other. The other *makes* me be. The examples show cases where the others *make* me be "facticity": certain predicates, such as Jew and baldhead, express this "social facticity." The *loving* encounter, however, does not *make* the other be "facticity" but "subjectivity." Love "creates" the subject. This does not mean, of course, that without the other's love I am not a subject. But the statement that I am a subject can have many meanings. It can indicate that I am not a thing, but also that I live in the fullness of authentic manhood. And in between these two, there is room for an entire scale of intermediary meanings. This point should be kept in mind when one tries to understand that love creates the other as a subject.

It is to be noted also that love's creativity may not be reduced to the efficacy of a deterministic cause in the sense of physical science. The reality of love, as it is accessible to us in our "lived" experience, cannot be expressed in physical concepts. The essential moments of love—appeal, destiny, availability, self-denial and acceptance—imply reciprocity and freedom; hence they are the very denial of unilateral and deterministic causality and cannot be "explained" through it.

Love's creativity is perhaps best understood through an analysis of being-loved. What does it mean that the other loves me? His loving turning to me *makes* my subjectivity *be* insofar as, through his affection for me, he mysteriously participates in my subjectivity: I no longer "alone" project my manhood and "alone" go forward to my destiny, but now do so "together" with the other. His love gives me to myself, gives me a certain fullness of being. Love's creativity is particularly evident in the bringing up of children. The parents' love raises the child, as it were, "above itself," their "power" of affection makes it become "master of the situation" and able to realize itself on a level which it would never have reached if it had been left "alone."

The realization that one is no longer "alone" testifies perhaps most eloquently for love's creativity. Love creates a "we," a "being together" that is experienced as wholly different from every other kind of "we." The "we" of love can only be expressed—if it can be expressed at all—in such terms as "fullness," "fulfillment," or "happiness."

My world also is re-created by the other's love. Through his love, the world shows its kindest face to me and becomes accessible for me in my self-realization: it becomes my "homeland," I feel at home in it and like it. Children whose parents are unfeeling psychopaths are destined to meet only the harshest meanings of the world. For them the world is only resistance, something which from their early youth inspires them to protest and revolt. Without love the world is hell for man.

Like love itself, however, the creativity of love is *situated*. It will be more or less creative according as my encounter with the other offers a greater or lesser opportunity to "will the other as a free subject." Some people I meet only in an incidental fashion, such as fellow travellers on a plane; with others I have frequent and more intimate contact, such as friends and family. Love's creativity will obviously be greater and manifest itself more strikingly in the loving "we" of the family than in that of a casual encounter.

The "influence" of love, we said, is not a causal influence in the sense in which this term refers to things. For the lover's creative affection only bears fruit if the beloved accepts this affection and makes it fruitful. The lover wills the other's subjectivity, his freedom and transcendence; he, therefore, can only will that the other *freely* consents to the love offered to him. The pedagogical situation is particularly illuminating here. The educator knows that his love is not understood if the person to be educated simply does what he says because the educator is "boss." Love is not a "causal influence" but a mysterious exchange between subject and subject.

To finish this section, let us add one more remark about the clear-sightedness of love. The "you for whom I care" is accessible to me on condition that I love the other. Neither physical science nor an objectivistic psychology can "verify" the reality of this "you." Only love "sees" it, and what I see is beyond dispute. The indisputable character of this "you"-reality can be understood to some extent now that we have seen that love is creative. For through love I "create" that which I see, I "make" the other "be" what I see. Thus it is impossible for one who does not love to see what the lover sees. This does not unduly disturb the lover, for he knows that "it is impossible to come to an agreement with one who is unwilling or unable to see" (Husserl).

6. JUSTICE

Any study of love, conceived as "humanity" *par excellence*, must also devote attention to justice. If justice is conceived as the willingness to abide by the legal order, one could easily show how much "humanity" there is in society because its members simply observe "the law." Strange as it seems, however, many jurists today refuse to identify justice with the legal order or to define justice in the usual way as willingness to abide by "the law." This fact is all the more remarkable because not too long ago jurists generally identified "right" with the positive legal order, and justice with the willingness to abide by the legal order; that is, they were legal positivists.

The Strength of Legal Positivism

In an era of internal peace the legal order can become almost sacrosanct, indisputable and definitive. Only the disadvantaged have the impression that the legal order is the product of arbitrary decisions made by the ruling powers. The law forbids, for instance, to beg near the entrance of a church, to steal bread or to sleep under bridges. All this is forbidden equally to both the rich and the poor.

After the chaos of World War II, however, the legal order in Europe was no longer held to be simply inviolable, for it had evidently been corrupted by the arbitrary decisions of those in power. New regulations appeared necessary, but on what basis could these regulations be made? Thus there arose again a call for the "natural law," which is the heart of the philosophy of law.

Legal positivism, however, remains an important phenomenon in the history of the philosophy of law, for, while rejecting philosophy of law, legal positivism presents itself as *the* philosophy of law and justice, *tout court*. It simply identifies "right" with the legal order, the rules laid down by law, custom, jurisprudence and the established institutions. Let us admit at once that legal positivism can offer strong arguments in its favor. Anyone should be sensitive to the idea that a society's value is in direct ratio to the value this society attaches to man's relationship with his fellowmen; anyone should be able to see how important the role is which the act of establishing a legal order plays in the actual humanization of human relations. There can be no question of justice—in the

185

provisional and vague sense of humanity—if the legal order itself is not explicitated as an essential aspect of justice, *tout court*.

To establish a legal order, power is needed, the power to impose and enforce decisions. One who clearly understands the demands made by the ideal of humanity but lacks the power to impose and enforce certain decisions does not *really* accomplish anything. He can preach humanity, but he cannot bring it about; he can hope for peace, but he cannot establish it. Because there is no humanity without a legal order, established by power, and because, generally speaking, the state has this power, one can understand that the legal positivist simply identifies justice with the readiness to carry out the demands of the state. Barbarism, the war of all against all, is more effectively contained by a primitive emergency law than by an ideal of justice.

Nevertheless, this cannot be the last word. History has taught us a terrible lesson. As late as 1932, the German legal positivist Gustav Radbruch wrote that he who holds the power to impose laws proves by that very fact that he is called to make the laws. The judge may merely ask himself what legally ought to be done, but not what is just. He must put aside his own sense of justice. Priests and ministers who preach against their convictions are despicable, but not so judges: a judge who does not allow himself to be sidetracked by his own sense of justice is praiseworthy.

Thus instructed the German legal profession entered the Third *Reich*. Theoretically legal positivism had already established that judges could not resist if the state issued an enforceable order to them to condemn all blue-eyed or hook-nosed children to death. After the fall of the Third *Reich*, legal positivism revealed itself as an hypothesis wrecked by the gruesome reality of history. The same

Radbruch, who had made the German jurists powerless in the face of Hitler, wrote in 1947 that the legal sciences should again reflect upon the age-old wisdom that there exists a higher right than the law, a "natural right," a "divine right," a "right of reason," and that injustice remains injustice as measured by this right, even if that injustice is given the form of a law.

One who identifies right with the legal order is *almost* right, and the same is true for one who identifies right with power. He is *almost* right and, therefore, he is *not* right.

The Untenable Character of Legal Positivism

Positivism, with its identification of right and the legal order, is untenable. First of all, laws are man-made, they are the work of man. Man makes laws *in order that there be justice.* This means that the making of those laws aims to establish "rights," in the provisionally still vague sense of "humanity." Right and law, therefore, cannot be identified.

Secondly, man continually revises the laws because he is convinced that the complex of laws contains also injustices. This does not mean that some laws go counter to other laws: they are unjust because they go against justice, against humanity. The laws are revised in order to bring them more into harmony with justice. This, again, shows that justice and law must not be identified.

Finally, it is possible—and it does happen—to manipulate the complex of laws in such a way that one can commit the greatest injustice with impunity. If justice and law were identical, such a possibility could not exist.

It is true, of course, that the positive sciences of law cannot ask any question about the justice or injustice of a law or legal order. But one who reflects upon positive law does not pursue a positive science but philosophizes about the law. He assumes an attitude of questioning which is fundamentally different from that of the positive sciences of the law. He considers fundamental questions which can never be answered by those sciences. The first of these questions is: what exactly is the principle or "right" that serves as an orientation point for the law and guides man to be just?

The Normative Character of the Legal Order

All jurists are convinced that the legal order *ought* to be observed. But why? Certainly not because there is a law prescribing obedience, for why ought such a law to be obeyed? The foundation on which the obligation of the entire legal order is based cannot be itself a positive law. Legal positivism, which identifies right and legal order, leaves the entire legal order without a foundation.

This same idea can also be expressed in a different way. The "willingness to comform to the demands of the legal order"—legal justice—presupposes man as a *subject*, and the "ought" ascribed to justice implies that this willingness is not left to the subject's arbitrary decision, but an attitude which is *obligatory*. If, then, being-a-subject *itself* does not imply a certain obligation, then it remains fundamentally unexplained why the legal order has an obligatory character. If the subject *himself* is not an "obligation," an "ought," then one can endlessly repeat that the legal order obliges, but this repeated assertion does not really mean anything. It is the subject, not the legal order, to whom a certain "ought" is inherent: he *ought* to be just.

We can now formulate the second fundamental question of the philosophy of law. It is concerned with the essence of the "ought" of justice, the obligation to do what

188

is right. The legal order is not identical with right; it sometimes goes even counter to it. In such a case justice requires man to reform or overthrow the legal order, for man "ought" to be just. This "ought" remains unexplained in legal positivism.

The "Inspiration" Underlying the Idea of the Natural Law

To anyone who is familiar with the history of the philosophy of law it is evident that the philosophical question about what right and justice are is identical with the historical question about the essence of the so-called "natural law." We will not hesitate to raise this question again, but let us add at once, we refuse to permanently fasten the use of the terms "natural law" and "natural right" to untenable conceptions of the natural law. At the same time, we also refuse to drop those terms themselves, for it does not make sense to reject terms merely because in the past they were used to express views which one cannot accept.

The historical use of the term "natural law" points to an "inspirational idea" in which the *humanity* of the legal order was the point at issue. The struggle about the natural law must be viewed as the search for a foundation and a critical norm of the legal order. Anyone who refuses to stop this search holds that there is a "natural law"; anyone who rejects this search is a legal positivist.

Even the most rigorous positivist, however, defends the absolutism of positive law because he cares for establishing humanity. According to him, the acceptance of the absolute validity of positive law and of the authority of the state is the only way to be "just." But according to those who claim that there are natural rights, precisely that absolutism makes it possible to do violence to humanity—a

189

violence of which history offers many examples. What, then, is this *humanity* for which both legal positivism and the defenders of the natural law are struggling?

Struggle Against Inhumanity

According to Hobbes, man in his natural condition is wholly guided by egoism. Life is dominated by a paralyzing fear of death because there prevails a war of all against all. "Man is a wolf for his fellowman." There simply is no question of sympathy, disinterestedness and love. The natural condition is identical with barbarism and inhumanity.

Similar ideas can be found in Spinoza. Religion teaches people that they should love one another, but in reality this teaching is not very effective in overcoming egoism, the lust for power, vengeance and honor of men, or their envy. In the church, people accept the doctrine of love, but where they have to deal with one another—in the market place and political life—there they try to destroy one another.

It is hardly necessary to mention that what Hobbes and Spinoza—or in our time Sartre with his philosophy of hatred—say about man's dealing with his fellowmen is part and parcel of reality, the reality of inhumanity and barbarism. Barbarism is more than a phase of history which is past in some parts of the world but still exists in others; it is a permanent aspect of man's *co-existence*. Our question here is whether barbarism is the whole "truth about man."

The "Origin" of "Natural" Rights

It seems undeniable to us that the inhumanity of barbarism is not the last word in human relations. At a particu-

190

lar moment in the history of certain societies there arose, through the intermediary of an "ethical genius," a "vision" of what it means to be man which, as a *matter of principle*, broke through the inhumanity of barbarism, that is, man's effective willingness to destroy his fellowmen as subjects. No such principle is involved when man, involved in a war of all against all, "sees" that this war can only terminate in the total destruction of "society" and therefore tries to stop barbarism by means of a "social contract" based on fear alone.

Undoubtedly, such a contract sometimes *de facto* establishes humanity, at least as long as neither party is able to destroy the other without crippling itself. But there is no transcendence of inhumanity as a matter of principle there until an "ethical genius" at a given moment of history "sees" man as essentially destined for the other, a destiny which he executes by his "yes" to the other's subjectivity. Man's being discloses itself to the "ethical genius" as a "having to be in the world for the other," and this disclosure imposes itself upon man with a *binding* force. For the "light" which the subject himself is is an objective light, a light which does not permit man to deny that which appears in this "light." Thanks to the "ethical genius," man "sees" that he himself *is* a certain "ought" with respect to his fellowmen, he "sees" that his very essence implies an orientation to the other. The execution of this "ought" is called "love," which is to accept, will, support and foster the other's subjectivity, selfhood and freedom.

Thus man appears to himself as a paradox. On the one hand, he is willingness to destroy the other's subjectivity, which is implemented in "hatred" or being a "wolf." On the other, he experiences himself as destiny for the other, which is implemented in "love." Experiencing himself as both "wolf" and "destined for his fellowman," man "sees," thanks to an "ethical genius" that the *minimum* demand contained in his being-destined-for-the-other consists in not permitting the "wolf" in him to devour the other.

The *minimum* demanded by love, then is formulated as the most fundamental right of the other. His right is the minimum of my "yes" to his subjectivity, a "yes" called for by my *existence* as a "having to be for the other," that is, as an "ought" on the level of *intersubjectivity*. The other's right thus is a "natural" right, better, an "essential" right, for it is contained in the "nature" or "essence" of man as *intersubjectivity*. By executing my "having to be for the other," I am *authentically* human. If I do not execute this "having to be," I am, in a certain sense, not man, that is, not authentically human.

Because the other is an embodied subject in the world, his "natural" right has two aspects. It is a "subjective" title to something because his subjectivity is the correlate of my "yes" to him as a subject. It has an "objective" side because the other is an embodied subject who needs part of the world in order to be himself.

All this is, of course, an abomination in the eyes of the legal positivist. His ire is caused by the seeming surrender of everything he calls "right"—in the sense of "law and order"—to the "subjectivism and relativism" of man's personal inspiration—all of it in the name of love! This alleged "subjectivism and relativism" will be discussed later; for the present we simply wish to emphasize that our position does indeed do away with the objectivism and absolutism of legal positivism. Positivism identifies justice with the willingness to abide by positive law and therefore *cannot* accept that justice would ever oblige man to overthrow the legal order. At the same time, positivism is unable to account for the "ought" it ascribes to this legal order. Such an account is possible only if man *him-*

self can be called a certain "ought" with respect to his fellowmen.

We have indicated this "ought" in the preceding pages. The legal order is normative because it embodies the minimum of man's "having to be for the other." But if this legal order itself does violence to the subject, then it is unjust for precisely this reason. The minimum of love man owes his fellowmen—that is, justice—then obliges man to overthrow, if necessary, the legal order. Justice is not the willingness to abide by the law but to respect rights, conceived as that which corresponds to the minimum implied in my "yes" to the other's *existence*.

Humanity, as the fundamental transcendence of barbarism is born from man's "yes" to his fellowman. Let us add that no sociological "we," no society, be it Marxist brotherhood or Western democracy, carries a guarantee that it will be human.

The Ethical Genius

It goes without saying that we do not conceive the objectivity of natural rights and duties in an objectivistic sense. To be objective is to be objective-for-a-subject. "The" subject brings about the truth of rights and justice, "the" subject "originates" the truth of *existence*. But, we must ask, who is this subject?

In our era things formerly done out of love by the best members of society are affirmed as rights. This fact indicates that at first "the" subjects for whom the demands of justice are objective are the best in that society and, after them, all others who, thanks to them, are able to "see" what the best "saw." Only the best "bring about" the truth of the demands of justice because only they see the other-as appeal-to-their-*existence* and themselves as "hav-

193

ing to be for the other." One who is immersed in greed or pride or one who will do anything that will enable him to realize himself as a "wolf" is simply unable to see the rights of the other. The "coming about" of the objectivity of rights presupposes an "ethical genius," one who at a given moment of history "sees" what the other's appeal and his own destiny for the other imply. And when he "sees," the truth of what he "sees" becomes objective, it becomes the objective meaning of being-man. The minimum of this humanity is formulated as the most fundamental right of the other.

Thus we must say that there are no natural rights "in themselves," rights which are immutable, eternal and valid for all "in themselves." Natural rights are made objective through an historical act of the "ethical genius." The latter, however, "brings them about" in the name of all human beings, he "brings about" a truth which is, in principle, intersubjective.

The important point here is not that the "ethical genius" brings about a truth that is, in principle, intersubjective. He would do the same if, suffering from a stomach ache, he would let that truth "come to pass," for all truth is, in principle, intersubjective. But in "bringing about" the truth and objectivity of natural rights, the "ethical genius" "brings about" the truth of man's *essence* as *intersubjectivity*, the truth by which man is authentically man, a truth which, in principle, applies to all people, at all times and in all places.

Because the minimum demanded by love is not something static, "seen" once and for all, the natural law is never "finished," but takes part in an endless history. If we keep this in mind, we realize that many human societies at many times and in many places live in many different phases of the natural law. It stands to reason that this situation causes great difficulties in the relations of different peoples.

Let us add that there is a standpoint from which the natural law is "eternal" and "immutable." Even though the truth of the natural law is an endless history, the "already" of the initial demand of justice can never be destroyed by the "now" of the same demand. What was "already" disclosed as a demand of the natural law cannot be discarded by, but only integrated in what is "now" disclosed. The other's right to live, for example, is not discarded by the fact that now we "see" also his right to old age security. In this sense the natural law is immutable. The same natural law is also "eternal," in the sense that something which, in any phase of the subject's history, has compelled him to really "see" and affirm it as an *essential* demand of *intersubjectivity* will compel him also to the same affirmation in any subsequent phase of his history. He can never deny the truth of that demand.

The Necessity of the Legal Order

The fact that an "ethical genius" "sees" the demands of humanity does not at all mean that by this very fact any kind of humanity is *established*. At first, "the heroes and the saints" who "see" stand alone, they are like a "voice in the wilderness" of inhumanity and barbarism. Although they make it possible for others to "see" what they themselves "saw" first, the fact that they "see" does not *establish* humanity: humanity does not yet "reign."

The demands of justice and right only become a *reigning* humanity when a positive rule of law, imposed with compelling force, is formulated as that which imposes itself as a demand of humanity in the encounter of man's "yes" to his fellowmen with the actually existing situation

195

and relations. In this way that rule then becomes embodied in those relations. This "process" of embodiment cannot be dispensed with. If the demands of humanity are not embodied in the existing relations by a compelling legal order, man would, at best, be "left to the mercy" of his fellowman's spontaneous love with its moments of weakness and, at worst, be thrown to the "tender mercy of wolves."

The legal order, therefore, is wholly indispensable for making the minimum of love "reign." The establishment of a legal order is a first step on the road to *effective* humanization of human society, the first success in taming the "wolf," the first victory over barbarism. The legal order takes the necessary steps to effectively establish humanity, it guarantees a certain stability to the humanity that has already been attained. This stability is the expression of a society's firm will not to sink below a certain level of humanity.

When spontaneous love and the "juridical attitude" are compared, it is easy to see that the "humanity" of love cannot hold a candle to the "humanity" of the legal order. One has only to visit a court of law where people are engaged in litigation. Love seems to be entirely absent. No matter how disgusted one is by such a sorry spectacle, however, one cannot remain insensitive to the fact that there is a minimum of "humanity" there thanks to the law: engaging in a lawsuit is a great advance over settling matters with fists and daggers.

Authority and Power

Laws cannot *compel* to humanity unless they are imposed by an authority having power. When an "ethical genius" "brings about" the truth of a natural right, it depends largely on the response of society whether or not this new form of humanity will actually be *established*. At first, there will be very few who "see" what the "ethical genius" "sees." Thus his primary task is to educate his fellowmen, to make them "see," so that they, too, will understand the demands of justice. As soon as this is sufficiently done, society will "elevate" one or more bearers of authority to make these rights become realities. These persons derive their authority from the "having to be" which *intersubjectivity* itself is and, on the basis of this "having to be," the rules which they establish are normative. And it is only to the extent that they represent this "having to be" that those persons are bearers of authority.

Historically speaking, our theory often means revolution against an oppressive situation and, philosophically speaking, the theory is a justification of such a revolution. In other cases, where it does not lead to a revolution, the person or persons "at the top" are forced to a "change of heart." By conforming to the demands of justice, a tyrant can become a legitimate bearer of authority.

To exercise authority, however, power is needed. This point also has been heavily emphasized by legal positivism, and justly so. To make justice and rights actually reign, power is essential—to such an extent that those who identify right and might are *almost* right. Humanity must become an accomplished fact, and this requires power. Those who dearly wish to make humanity reign but never have been tempted to identify might and right do not yet understand that the actual reign of humanity cannot be established by mere expressions of love.

Our own era makes us painfully aware of this truth. There exists no significant body of international law because there exists no supranational authority. One who would like to consider the United Nations as such an authority cannot ignore the fact that the action of this organization will remain weak as long as it does not have its own supranational armed forces. Radical pacifists and anti-militarists also make a mistake when they deny the importance of power. They are for a just peace, but without armies; they want right without might. This is a utopian view, which blissfully disregards the "wolf" in man.

The "Pressure" of the Legal Order as a Quasi-process

Speaking of *existence* as *co-existence*, we emphasized that man is whatever he is through others. The group makes the individuals think, act and be. This quasi-process of making one another *be*, however, is an indispensable condition for an authentic, personal *existence*. The group's "pressure" establishes in the individuals a "social body," so that the "soul" of authentic, personal *existing* can emerge. Without this "social body," no individual *existence* can reach any level of authenticity.

This idea applies eminently to the legal order as materialized humanity. The legal order itself is a part of man's "social body," of his facticity. The law "runs its course" and "functions" and those who live in a society experience its "pressure." If anyone tries to disregard the legal norm and escape from its "pressure," the law "proceeds" against him in a trial in which legal justice is blindfolded.

It is very important that the members of a society undergo the "pressure" of the legal order. For this "pressure" establishes in them a materialized humanity, the achievements already attained in past struggles against the "wolf" in man, even though they themselves have had no share in those struggles. They can lead a life that is, at least to some extent, human, but they owe this at first to the fact that they *themselves* do not live but "are lived." In a legal order many live on a relatively human level—a level which they would never reach if they *themselves* had to be just.

Is This View Anti-personalistic?

Does the accent which we place here on the importance of undergoing the "pressure" of the legal order, conceived as materialized humanity, imply a denial of authenticity? Is our view anti-personalistic? In reply, we would like to re-emphasize the mutual implication of subjectivity and facticity. The subject can be authentically himself only on the basis of his social facticity. It is the social facticity, the "social body" he has received from others that makes it possible for the subject to be authentically himself. Note, however, that we say "makes it possible" for him to be authentically himself. For one could legitimately ask: how many people are there who really *exist* as authentic selves, as authentic subjects? How many are ready for so much humanity that *of themselves* they do what is prescribed by the law?

Anyone knows that in every society there are always many who do not reach the level of humanity attained by the "ethical geniuses" whose vision gave rise to the legal order. For this reason it is good that *all* members of society undergo the "pressure" of the legal order. The "reign" of the law gives all of them a social facticity whose "weight" "drives" them to a particular way of behaving toward their fellowmen. This "weight" is materialized humanity. In its turn, this weight "produces" humanity in the members of society.

Such a view is not anti-personalistic, but simply recognizes the undeniable fact that, although all men are called to the authenticity of being-just, many do not attain it. Accordingly, the term "just" can have a full scale of meanings. The "ethical genius" is just, but one can also

say that the young criminal is just, who has learned from
his father that the police never gives up on murder and
who therefore carefully abstains from that kind of crime.
That, too, is important. If only mankind had some kind of
international police, the fear of which would keep nations
from taking each other by the throat.

Mutability of the Legal Order

Neither the inspiration of love nor the actually existing
relations and conditions of society are fixed entities. Thus
it should be obvious that the legal order must be continually revised.

The legal order embodies, we said, the *minimum* demands of love, and this means that "the best of society"
are unable to be satisfied with whatever results have already been achieved. Love knows no limits; hence the
legal order is never "finished." Every forward step on the
road to humanization discloses new perspectives of
greater humanity. Thus the "seeing" of the "ethical genius" is an unending history. The implications of being-
destined-for-the-other only become evident in the history
of man's effective love for his fellowmen.

An "ethical genius" is needed in a primitive society to
induce this society to abolish the burning of widows together with their deceased husbands. But the idea of
humanity needed for this is not so transparent that one
can also see in it the widow's right to a pension or old age
security. The view that there exists such a right required
a long history of humanization. It is within history, not
outside or above it, that the idea of justice really lives.
Because this history is never finished, there is room for
"inventions" also in the realm of justice.

As soon as an "invention" is made in the realm of what
humanity demands, the legal order becomes antiquated,

in the sense that it embodies only a phase in humanity's history which has already been overcome in the lives of the "best of society." If it is not changed then, the legal order becomes an obstacle to the authentic life of *co-existing* men.

The legal order has, of course, also and of necessity a static aspect, for this order must establish the *security* of human rights. Exclusive attention to this static aspect, however, could make man lose sight of the origin and purpose of the legal order. It can happen that laws and legal institutions begin to lead, as it were, a life of their own and that jurists handle them as if they were autonomous entities. The "justice" of such jurists is only capable of settling "old debts" (Nédoncelle); it lacks all creativity. A petrified legal order can be an obstacle to the attainment of greater humanity.

The fact that the minimum of love continually changes makes it possible to understand that former "acts of charity" are now demands of justice: what the "best" did out of love the legal order now demands of everyone. Let us add that traditional morality has always considered obligations of justice greater than those of charity or love. This stands to reason, for man has a greater obligation to the minimum than to that which goes beyond the minimum.

The actually existing social conditions are extremely important with respect to the establishment of a legal order. One who relies solely on the "inspiration" of love can only build a "castle in the clouds": he fails to put order in the actually existing conditions because he has no realistic understanding of these conditions. When these conditions change, then the legal order itself must also be modified. Otherwise real life outgrows the man-made structure of the law, with all the terrible consequences this can have. The supporters of the *Ancien Régime* and

201

of liberalistic capitalism tried in vain to contain the changed conditions within the structure of a static legal order. Some colonizing nations endeavored to do the same, and one or the other still keeps trying to do this. Such an effort is doomed to ultimate failure.

The same idea applies also in the more modest realm with which law makers and jurists deal in their everyday work. As soon as the rights and duties about a particular subject matter have been laid down in laws, things happen in the actually existing conditions which make new measures necessary. For example, by the time that an industrial safety code had finally been set up on the basis of steam engines as a source of energy, industry switched to electricity, thereby necessitating a complete overhaul of that code. Similarly, man's right to traffic safety calls for different regulations depending on whether a society uses donkeys, bicycles, motorcars or jets for its transportation.

The Necessity of Love

From all this it should be evident that Marx's theory about the history of humanity is one-sided. In his theory the objective reality of the proletariat produced by the process of capitalism leads deterministically to the Communist future of universal brotherhood and justice, independently of anyone's subjective intentions and dispositions toward his fellowmen. Love plays no role whatsoever in this. The capitalistic legal order simply mirrors the actually existing conditions of exploitation and injustice, but the Communist legal order will mirror the justice of man's universal recognition of man. Marx, however, could only call the capitalistic order unjust because he saw this order as a violation of his fellowmen's subjectivity, because he had personally said "yes" to his fellowmen's subjectivity, because he loved his fellowmen. But this inspiration of Marx's entire life does not occur in his philosophy.

In conclusion, then, the mutability of the legal order does not find its explanation in love *alone* or in the changed conditions *alone*. It is in the encounter of these two aspects of human *co-existence* that the necessity to make new laws makes itself known.

Suggested Readings

Luijpen, *Existential Phenomenology*, Chapter Four.

Remy C. Kwant, *Phenomenology of Social Existence*, Chapter Two.

Sartre, *Being and Nothingness*, Philosophical Library, New York, Part Three, Chapters 1–3.

Marcel, *Being and Having*, Torchbooks, Harper and Row, New York, N. Y. *Metaphysical Journal*, Rockliff, London, 1952.

M. Nédoncelle, *Love and the Person*, Sheed and Ward, New York, 1966.

Emmanuel Levinas, *Totality and Infinity*, Duquesne University Press, 1969.

Hans Kelsen, *Pure Theory of Law*, University of California Press, Berkeley, 1967.

Thomas Hobbes, *Leviathan*.

Spinoza, *A Political Treatise*.

CHAPTER FIVE

The Metaphysical in Man

THE CENTRAL REFERENCE POINT of existential phenomenology is for us *existence* or intentionality, conceived as the subject's openness to everything which is not the subject himself. "Everything which is not the subject himself" includes, as we saw, the world, in which the subject is consciously involved, and the other subject, for whom he is destined. Does the subject's openness extend to anything else? We may not arbitrarily and *a priori* exclude an affirmative answer by saying that man is *nothing but* a being-in-and-"at"-the-world, thus eliminating even the possibility of an authentic "affirmation" of a transcendent reality or God. Safeguarding this possibility, however, by the above-mentioned openness to "*everything* which is not the subject himself" does not absolve us from the duty of critically investigating whether and to what extent the "affirmation" of God is tenable.

Let us add at once that it is almost impossible today to say anything about either the "affirmation" or the "denial" of God without fear of being misunderstood. Sincere atheists cannot state their atheism without seeing their writings "interpreted" by certain theists to "prove" that those atheists "really" are theists. Others claim that those theistic "interpreters" can deliver their "proofs" only because they themselves lack any idea of what an "authentic" "affirmation" of God means. Others, again, claim that

204

"God is dead"—not just that our *image* of God is no longer viable, but God Himself is dead. Yet, they refuse to be called "ordinary" atheists, for, so they say, God did exist at one time, but now He is really dead. Finally, there are people who assert that God exists, but they are unmasked as atheists.

To a certain extent this confusion is inevitable. It is, indeed, possible, for example, that one who affirms God really affirms only a pseudogod. The confusion, however, seems greater than necessary because the presuppositions of both the "affirmation" and the "negation" of God often remain insufficiently examined. The result is that many people do not realize what they themselves or others affirm or deny.

A full examination of all questions connected with the "affirmation" and "denial" of God would require a large volume. Thus only some points can be touched here. Let us begin with a description of the "actual state of the question."

1. MYTHS

For Auguste Comte myths belong to the first stage of development of the human mind. In this stage man uses only his imagination, connecting the phenomena of nature with God, gods or spirits. He invents myths to explain things. This invention is important because it means that man *tries* to find explanations, and if he did not try to do this, he would never reach the stage of maturity, that is, of scientific explanation. Once the mature stage is reached, however, there will be no room for myths and their "affirmation" of God. Comte, then, rejects myths in order to posit his "negation" of God. The same holds for other adherents of scientism.

Comte's expectations, however, have not been filled.

Myths have not disappeared and for the past fifty years they are no longer being interpreted as mere "fiction." Today we try to take the myths as they were understood in primitive societies and we have gradually begun to see that a standpoint is possible from which myths are "true."

Rudolf Bultmann occupies a special place in this new vision of myths because of his program of "demythologizing." His program intends to let the "affirmation" of God have its own truth. For this "affirmation" has always made use of myths; hence, if myths are not understood according to their own "truth," they falsify the "affirmation" of God.

For Bultmann, the atheist is right when he refuses to affirm God if such an affirmation would demand of him that he accept as an *historical* or a *scientific* truth something which cannot possibly be verified by the methods of the sciences of history or physical science. Bultmann, however, only rejects myths insofar as they are falsely interpreted—that is, held to be true in the sense of physical science or that of the sciences of history, without being subject to the verification methods accepted in those sciences. Unlike Comte, then, Bultmann does not posit the "negation" of God, but only claims that the "affirmation" of God has a unique and distinct character of its own.

Bultmann's reason for rejecting myths in the above-mentioned scientific interpretation is not that their content is *de facto* not verifiable by those sciences, but that that content is in principle inconceivable by those sciences. In the domains of the physical and historical sciences it is simply inconceivable that one accepts the specific laws governing those domains and, at the same time, does not accept them by positing that God sometimes overrides those laws. Moreover—and this is more important—one who affirms the possibility that God overrides the scientific and historical laws thereby shows that he conceives

God as a worldly reality and no longer as a transcendent God.

It may be useful to add that the view which represents God as a factor "puncturing" the laws of nature and of history is sometimes called "supernaturalistic," "metaphysical" or "theistic." As we will see, however, these terms can be used in a different context and then have a broader sense than the one referred to here.

Bultmann, in rejecting the false interpretation of myths, argues that what the myths really intend to express must be brought to light. He holds that what they intend to speak of is the essence of man as *existence:* they must be interpreted existentially. The "objectifying" thinking of the sciences and history does not exhaust man's reflection upon himself. In the myths man does not occur as an element of history or of nature, but the myths intend to speak of man's authentic reality, his understanding of his *existence.* They try to give expression to the idea that it belongs to man's essence to recognize that the world in which he lives does not have a ground and purpose in itself and that man is not his own master. But myths "objectify" the Transcendent as the "world here": contrary to their real intention, they represent the Transcendent as the spatially distant and His power as rising above and exceeding human power. It is precisely to express the most profound dimension of man's "understanding of his *existence*" that myths use the term "God."

In line with all this is the view of those who see mythical speech as the *only* way in which God and things divine *can* be spoken of, provided this speaking correctly understands itself. This is only then the case, some thinkers hold, when one sees mythical speech as "bringing about" the essence of *existence* as orientation to the Transcendent. In mythical speech man does not speak "about" his *existence* or "about" God, but he "brings about" his *exist-*

ence and "confesses" God. Mythical language is the language of proclamation. This is also the reason why there are false myths: there are proclamations which mislead, disorient, point to a way that leads nowhere.

2. METAPHYSICS

The "actual state of affairs" also shows that there are many different standpoints with respect to metaphysics. Some thinkers reject metaphysics and, consequently, the possibility of "affirming" God. This is the standpoint taken by many adherents of analytic philosophy. For Ayer this standpoint implies that one should not only reject theism but also atheism and agnosticism, for the statements of the atheist and the agnostic also are metaphysical statements and therefore meaningless.

The reason why metaphysical statements are meaningless is that they claim to refer to a suprasensual world. Such statements cannot be verified—in the way Ayer understands this term—consequently, they are meaningless. Verifiable are only *a priori* or tautological statements— which do not lead anywhere—and empirical statements, based on observation of nature. But if the statement "God exists" is reduced to the affirmation of a certain regularity in nature, the believer objects that what he wishes to "affirm" is a transcendent being. In other words, it is beyond verification and neither false nor true but meaningless. The same applies to the statement, "God does not exist." Thus agnosticism is also condemned. The agnostic, says Ayer, admits that either the statement, "There is a transcendent God," or "There is no transcendent God" is true, but he cannot determine which one. The agnostic should see that both statements are nonsensical, for neither one nor the other can be verified.

Other thinkers, however, reject metaphysics with the

avowed intention of letting the "affirmation" of God have its own truth. They "confess" God but reject a "metaphysical affirmation of God." This expression can have various senses, which should not be confused. First of all, there is the "metaphysical affirmation of God" in the idealistic sense, to which we referred in Chapter One. The subject's relative priority is made so absolute that the Subject's qualities finally agree with the attributes traditionally ascribed to God. The Absolute Subject is then considered to act in and through the "little" subject. What actually happens, however, is that the little subject claims to think with "divine" authority and to act with a "divine" guarantee. Precisely for this reason, some thinkers reject the "metaphysical affirmation of God"; it fails to do justice to the authentic character of the "affirmation" of God.

Secondly, there is the "metaphysical affirmation of God" which is sometimes called "supernaturalistic" or "theistic." Its rejection can perhaps best be understood as a rejection of the consequences flowing from the Cartesian idea of God. Descartes began by reducing the *human* body, the *human* world and God-for-*man* to the *idea* of the body, the world and God. He realized, of course, that in this way he had not given expression to the "whole" *reality* of the human body, the human world and God-for-man, for they are "more" than ideas. Descartes, therefore, conceived what the body, the world and God are over and above ideas in an "inhuman" way as the body *in itself*, the world *in itself* and God *in Himself*. The affirmation of such a God-in-Himself is often called the "metaphysical," "supernaturalistic" or "theistic" affirmation of God that must be rejected in order to safeguard the authentic "affirmation" of God.

Such a "metaphysical God" can also be found in the objectivistic philosophy of order proposed by Scholasticism. As we saw, in this philosophy every essence, that of man included, was given a place in brute reality, and the "totality of reality" was conceived as a collection of essences which are necessarily, universally, immutably and eternally "true-in-themselves" because and to the extent that they are created by God. But one who conceives the order of being as "divorced" from man, implicitly also conceives its Creator as a God-in-Himself, a God with whom, *in principle, man has no relationship whatsoever.* God is the Transcendent-in-Himself, "metaphysically out there." One who still "believes" in the self-revelation of such a God is then forced to conceive his belief in such a way as to accept on authority the "truth" of judgments, statements or "articles" of faith about God, understanding their "truth" as their agreement with God-in-Himself. This is the position which some thinkers reject when they reject the "metaphysical," "theistic" or "supernaturalistic" God. In this sense Marcel exclaimed: "Theodicy, that is atheism!" But those who deny such an "inhuman" God do this only in order to be able authentically to "affirm" God-for-man.

The "metaphysical affirmation of God" is even more vehemently opposed by others when they observe that the "affirmation" of God as Cause does not differ from the affirmation of causes made by the sciences. As soon as metaphysics wishes to be a "science" to maintain its self-respect before the sciences, as soon as it calls the "Supreme Being" the "First Cause" in the way the sciences speak of causes, it represents God as the first cause in a series of causes. We must admit that the denial of such a "metaphysical God" comes closer to the "divine" God than does the affirmation.

Those who reject the "metaphysical affirmation" of a God-in-Himself also reject "metaphysical" agnosticism with respect to the affirmation of God. They point out that

THE METAPHYSICAL IN MAN

this agnosticism, which is defended, for example, by Karl Jung, is based on the same objectivistic ideal as the "metaphysics" which they cannot accept.

Finally, mention must be made of those thinkers who do not consider it necessary to reject the "metaphysical affirmation of God" in order to defend the "affirmation" of the "divine" God. They do not interpret metaphysics in an idealistic, objectivistic-realistic or scientistic sense, but simply consider all such interpretations degenerations of an authentic metaphysical inspiration. They defend a "human" metaphysics and the possibility of a metaphysical "affirmation" of the Transcendent God-for-man. In their eyes, the recognition of man's deepest dimension as an intentional being is identical with the "affirmation" of God-for-man. For them, the "proof" of God's existence simply explicitates the being of man as orientation to the Transcendent.

This extremely concise survey of the "actual state of the question" allows us perhaps to conclude that there exists a certain "trend" in man's thinking about God. Negatively expressed, this trend says that it is impossible to ask as a meaningful question—to be answered with a yes or no—whether or not God exists, unless the question is preceded by an inquiry into the possibilities and impossibilities of the "saying" of *is* which man himself is as an intentional being. This means that contemporary thought rejects the scholastic and Cartesian "affirmation" of a God-in-Himself. Hardly anybody today, however, fears that the "affirmation" of God-for-man is a form of atheism.

Positively expressed, the actual state of the question in man's "speaking about God" indicates the necessity of what Heidegger calls a "fundamental ontology" when he speaks about the meaning of Being. To express what the

211

believer means when he uses the term "God" is to give expression to the depth of man's essence as an intentional being, a being-to-the-other-than-himself.

There are several ways in which this can be done, so that the limited scope of this book imposes the necessity of making a choice. Let us emphasize at once that the choice we made does not deny the possibility and fruitfulness of a different approach. We would like to give new life to the traditional inspiration of metaphysical thinking, in the hope that we can manage to show that a renewed interpretation of this inspiration will be fruitful also for contemporary thought. At the same time, and more or less *en passant*, we can reply to those thinkers who believe that phenomenology makes metaphysics impossible. We will also devote a few words to Sartre's arguments that the existence of a God would make man's freedom impossible.

3. The Subject as the "Saying"-of-Is and Metaphysics

In Chapter Two we showed how and on what conditions reason can rise to the level of science. Anyone who pursues positive science starts with presuppositions which do not become the theme of his considerations because they are of a philosophical nature. For example, the simple fact that physical science formulates certain specific laws about things of nature presupposes that the being of these things is such that it can be approached by means of those laws. The physicist does not justify his presupposition; he does not formulate a philosophy of things of nature as such, but this philosophy is implied in the way he pursues his science. Similarly, by following as closely as possible the method of physical science, the psychologists of the past revealed their implicit conviction that man could be conceived as just another thing of nature.

Today it is explicitly recognized that, within the pursuit of the sciences, philosophical affirmations are executed. Positivism is losing ground to make room for authentic metaphysical—that is, philosophical—thinking.

For the great metaphysicians of the past, however, metaphysical thinking was more than the explicitation of the philosophical presuppositions of positive science. They viewed metaphysics as the ultimate possibility of human questioning and answering, as the question about the ultimate meaning of being: what *ultimately* does it mean that everything which is, no matter what, is said to *be?* Man uses the little word "is" most of the time unthinkingly. He takes for granted that being *is* and seems to know what he is saying when he says of anything that it *is.* This unquestioned obviousness, however, is merely a form of thoughtlessness. As soon as man ceases to take being for granted and asks himself what he is saying when he affirms of anything that it *is,* metaphysical thinking, in the strict sense of the term is born. Why is there something rather than nothing?

Affirmation in Negation

One who rejects metaphysics must begin by indicating what, in his view, is defended by the metaphysician. He will say, for example, that the results of such a way of thinking cannot be verified (Ayer) and conclude that metaphysical thinking is not concerned with anything.

It is obvious, however, that such a rejection of metaphysics implies a metaphysics. The rejection says that what cannot be verified—in the way the rejector understands this term—is simply nothing. "Something," then, is that which is verifiable in a certain way; "nothing" is that which cannot be verified in that way. There is here an implicit doctrine about something as something, about being as being, that is, as opposed to nothing. Thus the very rejection of metaphysics is also a metaphysics. For this reason even the most fervent opponents of metaphysics figure in surveys of metaphysics with just as much right as the defenders of metaphysics.

Metaphysics as Speaking About "Everything"

Metaphysics, in the strict sense, we said, is the attempt to express the meaning of being *as* being. Man can only say that particular beings are because he understands being *as* being. This point is the theme of metaphysics in the strict sense. Metaphysics is not concerned with "this" or "that" individual being but with the ground on which it can be said of individual beings that they *are*.

It should be clear now in what sense metaphysics speaks about "everything." Metaphysical thinking, in the strict sense, is the attempt to com-prehend "everything" in a single rational grasp. In metaphysical thinking, in the broader sense—in the philosophizing which is implied in the pursuit of positive science—there is also an attempt to arrive at a com-prehending, but it consists in the orderly arrangement of specific objects into a specific region of being, in which these objects agree with one another. For example, a metaphysics of the things of nature inquires into the meaning of the thing of nature *as* a thing of nature. The question about the meaning of the thing of nature abstracts from the fact that *this* thing of nature is a grass seed or a geological layer; at the same time, by man's com-prehending rational grasp all things of nature are, as agreeing with one another, constituted into a single region of being, distinct from other regions. In this way "regional ontologies" (Husserl) can be developed.

The thematization of the most fundamental presuppositions, however, is the task of metaphysics in the strict sense of the term. This metaphysics asks what exactly is affirmed when man on any level whatsoever says of anything whatsoever that it "is," that it "truly" and "really" *is* and not *not-is*. This metaphysics, then, is concerned with the saying of "is" *as such* and with being *as such*, it is concerned with what is traditionally called "the question of being."

Metaphysics in the strict sense must therefore be said to speak of "everything," but this expression must not be misunderstood. The metaphysician does not let his gaze wander over plants, planets, rocks, machines, rivers, mountains, cats and men in order to say something about each of them. Speaking about "everything" is only then an intelligent form of speaking when the speaking subject occupies a standpoint from which a certain com-prehending becomes possible, and this com-prehending must be such that it grasps whatever *is* as agreeing with all that *is*, excluding only nothing.

"The Metaphysical in Man"

The metaphysical question is not an invention of metaphysics as a "science," but is a mode of being-man. The knowing subject himself is "metaphysical consciousness." Metaphysical consciousness is a kind of "knowing" of what it means that everything of which it has been, will be, or is being said that it *is* belongs to reality, the order of being. In metaphysics this consciousness is taken up in a critical and systematic fashion, made explicit and developed. Metaphysics, then, is based on a dimension of the

215

subject's immediate presence to present reality, viz., the dimension in which the subject dwells in the universe, the universality of all beings as beings. Thus metaphysics presupposes "the metaphysical" in man, and for this reason it presupposes a philosophical anthropology and criteriology.

The phenomenological conception of reason leaves no room for an objectivistic metaphysics. People for whom objectivism is a necessary condition for authentic metaphysics will claim that phenomenology can never develop a metaphysics. But for a phenomenologist an objectivistic metaphysics is a contradiction. Metaphysics can only exist within the sphere of intentionality. For one who recognizes this, a "first" answer can now be given to the question, "Why is there something rather than nothing?" There is something because man is, the man who, as "metaphysical consciousness," lets "come to pass" the being of all that is and "brings about" the truth of being as being. This, however, is only a "first" answer.

4. The Existence of God

"Why is there something rather than nothing?" A "first" answer to this question is, as we saw, because man is: as metaphysical consciousness, man lets "come to pass" the being of all that is, he "brings about" the truth of being as being. There is, however, also a "second" answer to this most fundamental question man can ask. Asking about the beings of his experience, man realizes that these beings *are*, yet they reveal themselves as not having a ground for their existence in themselves.

These beings *are* not by virtue of their own essence, for otherwise they would be *pure* "to be." It is obvious, however, that they are not pure "to be," for they are *many*. The very fact of being *many* implies that they are different, for to be different can only mean that one has something which the other does not have; otherwise they would fully coincide and not be many. Hence the "to be" of these beings evidently implies a certain "not to be"; consequently, they are not pure "to be," but merely *have* "to be."

As soon as one realizes that these beings *are*, but *not* by virtue of their own essence, he also sees that they must be by virtue of *something else*, for there is no escape from the fact that they *are*. They are, in the classical term, "contingent."

To be by virtue of something else is the same as being by the influence of something else, the same as being-caused. Contingent beings reveal themselves as caused beings. Care must be taken, however, that the search for their cause does not get onto the wrong track. Asking about the cause of contingent being as being is not like asking: why are there lice in the vineyard? The attitude or standpoint one assumes in asking about a cause codetermines the kind of causal influence about which an answer is sought. The answer is valid for the region of being in which that causal influence applies, but not outside it.

Now, the metaphysician cannot be satisfied with any kind of causal influence belonging to a *particular* region of being. The biologist who explains why there are lice in the vineyard merely explains why the lice won a battle over the chemical spray; he does not explain that a battle was won over non-being, and he should not even attempt to explain this, for such a question is meaningless for him as a biologist. It is the metaphysician's task to explain why beings are in spite of their contingency.

What could possibly be the cause why contingent beings *are?* Certainly not any being that belongs to the universe, for anyone of them itself is a contingent being, a

217

caused being. This means that the universe, the universality of all beings, does not have a ground of being in itself. But the universe *is;* it is, therefore, by the influence of something else, and this "something else" cannot possibly *not be*, for then there would be nothing at all.

Affirmation or Negation?

At this juncture we realize that the contingent character of the beings of the universe has made us accept the existence of an Origin and Cause of these beings outside the universe, a Transcendent Origin or Cause. One cannot affirm the existence of contingent beings and, at the same time, deny the existence of the only Ground on which these beings can exist. This Transcendent Origin is known as God.

Can we really say that God *is?* The metaphysician realizes that he must say, "God 'is' "; yet it is impossible for him to say it unreservedly. The reason is that he uses the term "is" to affirm contingent being. By unreservedly using the same term, he would seem to affirm Transcendent Being as a contingent being, which is the only being of which he can form a direct concept. Man's thinking and speaking do not reach God in the same way as they reach the contingent beings of his experience. He can grasp these beings in concepts, but with respect to God the only concept he can have is a *directional* concept, a concept that is, as it were, a road sign, indicating which direction one should go. The road sign itself, however, does not go where it points. More concretely expressed, every "affirmation" of God must be accompanied by a "negation": God "is," but He "is not" as a contingent being is. To find Him, one must look in the direction of "is," and not in that of "is not." Or, to use another example, "God is a personal God" means: to find God, one must go in the direction of the person, and not in that of things.

The "proof" for God's existence, then, is not a demonstration, ending with "There He is," but merely a "way," indicating in what direction God must be sought. In the "proof" God does not manifest *Himself* to man, He does not become a "datum," something "given." For this reason atheism remains a fundamental human possibility.

Contemporary Objections to the "Proof"

Even when any trace of physicalism is removed from the "proof" for God's existence—as was done in the preceding pages—it does not escape objections from both believers and unbelievers. Let us begin with those of the believers.

The believer's complaint is that the "proof" does not satisfy the demands of man's authentic religiousness, it does not conclude to the reality which God is for the religious man, a God whom he can love and to whom he can pray (Marcel). Instead of that real God, the "proof" presents us with a Transcendent Origin or Pure "To Be." The God of the "proof," then, means nothing to the religious man and he can do without it.

Undoubtedly, it is true that for the man of faith God means much more than Transcendent "To Be," just as "my mother" means much more to me who love her than to the biologist who limits his considerations to the fact that I was conceived in her womb. In this respect we must agree with Marcel's objection. On the other hand, however, if my life as a believer in God is to be authentically human, it must have a rational justification; in other words, I must be intellectually convinced of God's existence. This conviction finds expression in the "proof" for God's existence—a proof which makes it impossible for me to deify myself or any other worldly reality because I realize that both I myself and worldly reality are not self-grounding.

The proof, then, helps remove the danger that I'll fall for a pseudo-god or reduce the Transcendent God to a worldly reality. To use again the comparison made above, I cannot express the reality which "my mother" is for me by pointing to a biological process, but this does not mean that this process does not belong to the integral reality which constitutes "my mother." It could even happen that only biology would be able to determine who is really "my mother." In a similar way it may happen that man needs metaphysics to determine who really is "his God." In this sense the "proof" for God's existence is neither super-fluous nor meaningless to the believer.

The above-mentioned objection of some believers in God to the "proof" for God's existence could also be for-mulated in a different way. The language of metaphysics, so it is said, in an objectifying, descriptive language, but the language of faith is the language of proclamation, confession and orientation. For this reason metaphysics cannot possibly speak of the God-for-the-believer, for an objectifying and descriptive language *per se* fails to say "enough."

That there is a difference between the objectifying and descriptive "language game" and other "language games" is rather obvious. The statement, "Fire! Fire!" does not intend to give an objective description of an actual condi-tion which in a particular culture is called "a fire," but means: "Stop what you are doing and help us." In other words, it is a call and not a description. In a similar way the language of faith is not descriptive but appealing, confessing, proclaiming and orientating. The statement, "Christ rose from his grave," intends to speak of something entirely different than the statement, "Christian rose from his deck chair."

Thus we must ask ourselves whether the philosopher *as* philosopher may *confess* God. In our opinion the answer is in the negative. There are, of course, and rightly so, philosophers who confess God, but they do not do this *as* philosophers. Irritating as this distinction is to many, it cannot be avoided, unless one wishes to cause misunderstandings that are entirely needless. All emphasis should fall, of course, on the terms "*as* philosophers" and "confessing" God. It stands to reason also that we do not wish to suggest that man can "divide himself into two" and that one half of him is a philosopher and the other half a believer. But is there any reason why the statement that I, *as philosopher*, cannot *confess* God *per se has to* be interpreted in such a silly way? To use a comparison, when it is said that the bacteriologist *as* bacteriologist cannot make any statement about the ethical evil of bacteriological warfare, no one insists that such a claim cuts the bacteriologist in two. The claim is accepted in order to prevent anyone from conceiving ethics as a branch of bacteriology. But bacteriologists have, of course, the right to explore ethical questions. If they do this, they do it as ethicists, however, and not as bacteriologists. In a similar way philosophers have the right to confess God, but they do this as believers and not as philosophers.

By virtue of its own, inner intention, the pursuit of philosophy resists confessing and proclaiming. The philosopher is first and foremost critical. He explores what is tenable in any statement whatsoever, including the confessing, proclaiming and orientating statement. This "reserve" of the philosopher is the reason why he, even if his critique happens to be positive, does not end up with more than the *descriptive* affirmation of what is offered to him as confession, proclamation and orientation. This is also the reason why politicians cannot do anything with philosophers. A political program is necessarily a "creed," a confessing, proclaiming and orientating program. The philosopher's answer to such a program is: "Let us have a look at it." But when he has critically "looked" at it and thinks that he can agree with it, his "confessing" has become a "describing," and no longer holds any attraction for the politician. The philosopher can, of course, also make political propaganda, but he cannot do this *as* philosopher. Philosophy *is* "reserve."

The same applies also to the relationship between philosophizing and the confession of belief. As soon as the philosopher *as such* explores this confession, there remains at most a *descriptive* affirmation.

Does all this imply that philosophy can be dispensed with or must even be rejected when there is question of speaking about God? In our opinion, this is not the case. Philosophy cannot be rejected or be dispensed with, even if it is true that the language of faith is confessing, proclaiming and orientating while that of philosophy is descriptive. Let us illustrate the matter by means of a simple example.

Riding through the country, I see somewhere on the window of a rural inn a sign: "The soup is ready to serve." Seeing this, I know that the sign does not simply observe and describe a fact but invites me to enter and take a meal if I am hungry. At home the soup is also often ready to serve, but no one puts a sign in the window to announce this fact. If one of the children would secretly put such a sign in the window, his mother would punish him because he plays a language game in which the mother does not wish to take part. For the language of the sign is a call, it invites and orientates, and it is not an objective report of an observable fact.

If, however, I enter the inn and the soup appears not to be ready to serve, the innkeeper cannot exonerate himself by saying that the language of the sign is "only" a call and an orientation and that it does not intend to be the objective description of an observable fact. For in that case we could rightly request him to show greater restraint in "calling" and "inviting." Because such things can happen, it is not meaningless if my companions ask me first to go inside and submit the language of the call and the invitation to a "verification." If I find out that the soup is really ready to serve, I communicate the result of my verification to my friends in descriptive language. This description does not have the meaning of a call or an invitation, but does that make the description meaningless? Obviously not.

This little story can perhaps serve to clarify the importance of philosophy for those believers who think that they can reject the "proof" for God's existence because it does not say enough. The philosopher "verifies" and he communicates the result of his "verification" in "descriptive" language. Note that the terms "verification" and "description" can also be used when, for example, I wish to classify insects, but in metaphysics they have a very special sense of their own. If we say that the metaphysician "verifies" and "describes," we solely wish to emphasize that he refuses to "confess" or "proclaim" anything, for the philosopher is "reserve" personified.

Believers and theologians, then, are right when they note that the metaphysician's descriptive speaking does not express reality as they confess it. It is true indeed that the metaphysician's descriptive speech does not say "enough." But they are wrong if they think that the metaphysician *intends* to say "just as much" as they themselves say. The metaphysician merely wants to "verify" in order to prevent everyone from "rushing in for the soup," even if "the soup is not ready to be served" at all. How often does it not happen that man is appealed to by "calls," "invitations" and "proclamations" whose *untrustworthiness* would at once be evident if people went to the trouble of "verifying" the *truth* presupposed by those "calls." The metaphysician does *not intend* to express reality as it is confessed by the believer. Accordingly, it is wrong to reproach the metaphysician for expressing what he really intends to express, in the mistaken assumption that he wishes to express the same as the believer intends. On such a basis it is easy triumphantly to conclude that the metaphysician is apparently unable to do anything else and that, therefore, what he is doing is devoid of importance for the believer. When there is question of attempting to speak of God, the metaphysician attempts the ultimate possibility of human reason, but this is *not faith*. He goes to the extreme limits of "descriptive" speech, but this is not a "confession."

The believer rightly emphasizes that the essence of "confessing" God is wholly unique and beyond the reach of the metaphysician. But if one appeals to this in order to disregard the demands of rationality, the uniqueness of the believing confession reveals itself as wholly insignificant. If the believer does not realize the outermost possibility of human reason, then his faith is not something "worthy" of man.

Atheism Among Those Who Affirm God's Existence

There is a good kind of atheism as well as a bad kind. Socrates' atheism was good because he rejected the pseudo-gods of Athens. He attacked the theism of the Athenians, but theirs was a bad kind of theism. As a negation of pseudogods, atheism is good and plays a much-needed purifying role. Let us examine some examples of bad theism, which had to be given up because of the critique of good atheism.

"Scientific" Proofs for God's Existence. At a time when many scientists rejected God because His existence could not be proved by physical science, a few "pious" scientists tried to formulate "scientific" proofs for His existence. Examples are Clausius' physical proof from the principle of entropy and the biological proofs of Carrel and Lecomte de Nouy.

Such kinds of proof, however, must *of necessity* fail, for they attempt to go beyond the fundamental possibilities open to positive science. These sciences are, in principle, limited to intraworldly realities and intraworldly causal connections. It is true, of course, that these sciences often meet enigmas in their research, dark corners. There is then a temptation to let the "light" of God shine into that dark corner and appeal to His influence as an explanation of the riddle. But the god hiding in the dark corners of science is always a pseudo-god, who will go the way of all pseudo-explanations when science makes progress. One can recall here, for example, the god of thunder and lightning, the sun god, the fertility gods. Within physical science there is room only for physical explanations based on measurement; when these measurements reveal a riddle, it is to be solved by other more accurate measurements, not by an appeal to a Transcendent God.

God does not appear behind a door opened by physical science; that door only leads to another physical problem clamoring for a physical answer. The metaphysician—or the theologian—does not take over when the physicist is "stuck" with a *physical* problem. When, for example, the physicists argue about the origin of primordial matter, the philosopher or theologian does not answer *their* question by speaking about the metaphysical question of creation. Creation is neither reconcilable nor irreconcilable with the results of physical science, for the simple reason that the "results" of physical science and those of metaphysics are unrelated, they do not move in the same orbit.

If it was shortsighted on the part of scientists in the past to reject God as a "superfluous hypothesis" and absolutely irreconcilable with the results of their science, it is just as shortsighted on the part of believers in God to claim that the present-day development of science demands the affirmation of God. The most one can admit is that today's science tends to make its pursuers less absolute in their claims and thereby creates a psychological atmosphere in which it is more difficult for the man who is a scientist to reject God absolutely on the alleged basis of his science.

Man No Longer Needs God. "God is absent" from the modern world, "as He has never been before" (Léon Bloy). Formerly, so it is said, man did not find it difficult to see God in the world. Man was so helpless that he was able to see God's providence in good health and illness, in prosperity and need, in good fortune and catastrophes. But today man is his own master; through his technology he has gained control over the world. Lightning no longer points to an angry God, is no longer an "act of God"; man's lightning rod does its job infallibly. When a calamitous flood inundates a city, man no longer considers that a divine punishment for his wickedness, but blames the lack of foresight of his engineers. To put it succinctly, man no longer feels the need of God because he has learned to save himself.

It would be dangerous to counter this argument by claiming that there are worldly needs, with respect to which man will always remain helpless and that, therefore, he needs God. Such a claim would run parallel with the claim that somewhere in a dark corner there are physical questions which can be solved only by an appeal to the existence of God. With respect to man's intraworldly needs, man's own powers are, in principle, unlimited. Moreover, claiming that any particular intraworldly need of man is beyond man's self-help and reserved for God is a dangerous procedure. It would lead to fatalism in the face of disaster and paralyze man's effort to free himself from such dangers to his self-realization. Besides, the demarcation of such a realm of needs beyond man's self-help would necessarily be marked by the possibilities that are *de facto* within man's vision at the *particular* period of history in which that realm would be delineated. It could, therefore, be overtaken by man's future development.

God is not absent from the modern world *because* man is now able to save himself through his technology; he was not present in the former world *because* more primitive people were helpless to satisfy their own needs. His alleged former presence was a pseudo-presence and his alleged present absence is a pseudo-absence. The only way God is present to any world, whether primitive or advanced, is as a transcendent Creator, as an "absent presence," that is, as a presence which is not the presence of an intraworldly cause. In today's highly developed culture it is no longer possible to present the affirmation of a pseudo-God as an authentic affirmation of God. Atheism has played a purifying role in this.

5. The Atheism of Sartre

We would like to finish this chapter by paying attention to Sartre's denial of God's existence. As could be expected, Sartre's atheism is based on his concept of human freedom. If God really existed, man could not be free. But it is an indisputable fact that man is free. Therefore, God does not exist. This one argument, however, is developed in different ways by Sartre.

God as the "Superior Craftsman"

Tradition, says Sartre, has always called God man's Creator and conceived his creation by analogy with the production of a thing by a craftsman. The craftsman first conceives what he wishes to make, the essence of the thing, in an idea and then makes the thing be as he has pre-fixed it in his mind. *In exactly the same way*, says Sartre, people speak about man's creation by God. God is a "superior craftsman," one who knows beforehand exactly what He will create and then gives man being in accordance with His idea. Thus God produces man just as the craftsman produces a letter-opener. Man's being is fixed beforehand and, because God's creation extends over the whole of man's life, man's entire life is fixed beforehand. In other words, man is nothing but a fixed sample of a fixed species, and his life is more or less like the growth and swelling of a pea.

Sartre rejects this doctrine because man would thus be nothing but a thing. The proper character of man, however, is that of *existence;* a self-realizing subject, as freedom, he gives meaning to his essence and in this way "makes" himself: "*existence* precedes essence." Accordingly, for Sartre the idea of a Creator God cannot be reconciled with the reality of man as freedom. Because man's reality is beyond dispute, no reality can correspond to the idea of the Creator God.

God as the Other par Excellence

Sartre's theory of intersubjectivity also make him reject God. God would be The Other *par excellence*. But this means that He is the one who "looks" at all subjects, the one before whom all subjects experience themselves as objects. God is the being who stares at every subject and Himself cannot be stared at: He is the "unstared stare." To accept God, then, would mean to accept being a thing, to accept my self-estrangement from my manhood-as-freedom. But man's freedom is not an illusion; therefore, he must reject God in order to remain free. Man owes it to his manhood to deny God.

In the light of what we have seen in Chapter Four about love and its creativity, it should be evident that both of these arguments are extremely one-sided. To begin with the second argument, it stands or falls with Sartre's claim that the only relationship between subjects is that of hatred, which tries to reduce the other to a thing. But if subjects can also love each other, then *The Other par excellence* could also be one who loves me, wills me as a free, self-realizing subject.

Regarding the first argument, it is wholly based on a univocal concept of causality which views all causality as the deterministic influence a thing exercises on a thing. It disregards the causality of love—which is not surprising because love plays no role in Sartre's philosophy. The lover also "makes" the other *be*, but, as we saw, love's "influence" respects the other's freedom. Thus it does not follow that if God is the cause of man, God's "influence" robs man of his freedom, for God's creativity with respect to man can be the creativity of love.

Let us add, however, that in the past philosophers and theologians very often spoke without sufficient discrimination about God's causality. It was conceived too much in a thinglike fashion. While recognizing that causality is an analogous notion, they failed to pay sufficient attention to the difference between the influence of a thing upon a thing and that of a person upon a person through love. It

229

is only in recent decades that stress has been placed upon
the "causality" or creativity of love. In this respect also
Sartre's critique of theism has played a purifying role.

The Idea of God as a Contradiction

Sartre also argues that the idea of God is a contradiction in terms. He makes use of his fundamental concepts
of the "in-itself" and the "for-itself" to establish this contradiction. The in-itself, as we saw in Chapter Two, *is* in
the full sense of the term, it is full positivity, fullness of
being and does not need anything else to be what it is.
This suffices, says Sartre, to show that the God spoken of
by religion must be an in-itself. For He is conceived as the
fullness of being, fully self-sufficient and not needing anything else to be what He is. At the same time, however,
religion conceives God as for-itself, as consciousness. But,
as we saw, consciousness or for-itself is diametrically the
opposite of the in-itself: the for-itself is nothing but negativity, it needs the in-itself to be able to be for-itself; hence
it is never self-sufficient.

The contradiction, then, is evident. God would have to
be the identity of the in-itself and the for-itself, of pure
positivity and pure negativity, of self-sufficiency and self-
insufficiency, of independence and dependence. The idea
of God, therefore, is a contradiction, so that no reality can
correspond to it.

This alleged contradiction, however, does not make
much impression on anyone who realizes what is happen-
ing here: Sartre abandons the reciprocal implication of
subject and object. What possible sense could be attached
to the "fullness of being" ascribed to the in-itself if one
accepts—as any phenomenologist does—that one can
meaningfully speak only of the in-itself-*for-us?* The in-it-
self-for-us, the thing-for-us, certainly does not appear as

fullness of being. Sartre fails to offer any justification for his sudden withdrawal of the phenomenological attitude of mind at this crucial point. In his opinion, the definition of God is a contradiction; actually, however, his own attempt to speak about the in-itself, reality as divorced from the subject, is a contradiction.

Similar remarks can be made with respect to the for-itself. Religion affirms that God is the Supreme Being and that, therefore, His being lies on the highest level of being, the level of consciousness. But Sartre denies all positivity to consciousness, thereby denying it the dignity of the highest mode of being. For him, consciousness is essentially negative, "nihilation." When religion conceives God as a conscious being, it does not "affirm" what Sartre affirms when he speaks of the for-itself. Religion conceives God neither as in-itself nor as for-itself in the Sartrian sense of these terms. What Sartre denies, then, is entirely different from what the believer affirms.

The Believer in God as the "Grave Man"

Sartre calls the man who adheres to God a "grave man." The grave man is a coward because he conceals his absolute freedom from himself. The grave man interprets his being as the being of a thing in the midst of things, he renounces his manhood in favor of the world of things. He ascribes to himself the being of a rock, the firmness and density of a thing-in-the-world. Because he refuses to face his own freedom, the grave man is in "bad faith."

Strange as it seems, according to Sartre, anyone who tries to be sincere is in bad faith. For what else is the attempt to be sincere but an effort to be for oneself what one is? Being what one is—that is exactly the definition of the *thing*. Such an effort is necessarily hypocritical, for man is not what he is but is what he is not. Man of necessity escapes from what he is; hence the ideal of sincerity is an impossible task.

The grave man, then, is in bad faith because he ascribes to himself the mode of being of a thing. This is exactly, says Sartre, what is done by the man who accepts God. Let us see what this means. The man who gives himself the mode of being of a thing depreciates his freedom as "distance," and this is precisely the reason why he is in bad faith. As we saw in Chapter Two, the distance inherent in the subject's involvement in facticity must be conceived in a twofold way. It contains "nihilation" on both the cognitive and the affective levels. The affective distance of the subject with respect to facticity is essential for his manhood. That is, it is wholly impossible for man fully and unreservedly to consent to any worldly facticity whatsoever: all fullness is permeated with emptiness, all rest, peace and happiness is mixed with unrest, trouble and unhappiness. When man fails to do justice to his non-being, to what he is not, he fails to do justice to his manhood; therefore, he is in bad faith.

This kind of man is rejected by Sartre, and justly so. Man cannot be satisfied with any form of his being-in-the-world; he cannot definitively and fully say "yes" to any worldly reality. And this is precisely what the grave man does. For this reason Sartre says that the grave man renounces his manhood in favor of the world and that he belongs to the world. Simone de Beauvoir, Sartre's most slavish follower, alluding to Nietzsche's superman, significantly calls the grave man a "subman." The subman loses himself to the object, he clings to his facticity and, consequently, blocks the enlargement of man's domain, the unfolding of his freedom. But the subman is bored and experiences the world as a desert. He is in bad faith.

It should be clear now what Sartre really rejects when he thinks that he is rejecting God. The man who accepts

God is "grave," but the grave man is one who renounces his manhood in favor of the *world*. God, then, is conceived as a worldly reality to which man gives his unreserved consent. Such a god must obviously and unconditionally be rejected by any believer in God, for such a god is not God. Simone de Beauvoir gives some unambiguous examples of the "gravity," that is, the acceptance of God, which she and Sartre despise so much: the soldier for whom The Army is everything; the colonist who sacrifices the natives to the building of The Road; the revolutionary who is blind to everything but The Revolution—all these are grave men because they are servants of "divinities." But what are these divinities but worldly realities to which an absolute value is assigned? He who unreservedly consents to them disregards the negativity affecting his *existence*, he crushes his freedom to death. But life will necessarily disappoint him, for his gravity is the impossible attempt to realize in himself "the contradictory synthesis of the in-itself and the for-itself." Simone de Beauvoir returns to this Sartrian definition of God immediately after giving the examples of "gravity."

The matter, then, is evident. God is conceived as a reality within the world, and the man who adheres to God is depicted as one who absolutizes his own relativity. It should hardly be necessary, however, to point out that all this has nothing to do with the true God and the authentic "affirmation" of God. One must even say that for a Christian to accept the Sartrian God would be a sin. Sin, in the strict sense of the term, is precisely the absolutizing of a worldly reality, an affirmation *à la* "grave man," and man's struggle against evil is precisely a struggle against the temptation offered by the world to make such an affirmation.

Sartre's way, however, of rejecting the subject's massive affirmation of the world is so penetrating that his insight into this matter may be called a permanent acquisition of philosophy. Perhaps no one else has ever thrown so much light on the fact that "having to be" constitutes the *inmost essence* of man. As long as man lives locked up in the world, it is impossible for him to definitively consent to his subjectivity as "having to be," for all consent to himself stands in function of the fulfillment which subjectivity as "having to be" finds. When man searches for a ground of his existence, he searches for a possibility enabling him to give a definitive consent to his subjectivity as "having to be."

Within the dimension of the world this is impossible. The grave man, the subman eloquently shows this. He is in bad faith, he is bored in a world, which for him is a desert. This boredom has a metaphysical dimension. It reveals to man the true character of subjectivity-in-the-world as a "natural desire" for more than worldly reality, a desire for something entirely other than the world. This "entirely other" Christianity calls the Transcendent God. God, however, is not a "reality" in the way the world is a reality. For this reason God can *never* be "affirmed" just as the world is affirmed. Any attempt to do this degrades God's transcendence and fails to do justice to the true dimension of the human subject as "natural desire."

Man is indeed a search for a possibility of definitively consenting to himself. On the basis of his "yes" to the world, it is not possible for the subject definitively to consent to himself, for his "yes" is essentially—and therefore, invincibly—affected by a "no." But, one could ask, would a "yes" to God be able to function as the foundation for man's definitive consent to his own subjectivity?

Within the perspective of Sartre's own *explicit* theories, this question is meaningless, for he rejects God; therefore, any definitive "yes" is for Sartre nothing but a form of estrangement. If, however, one *radically* distinguishes

God from the world, it will at least be impossible to claim that a definitive "yes" to God implies "gravity." The grave man, it should be recalled, unreservedly affirms the *world*. His affirmation cannot give meaning to life but makes it a "useless suffering" (Sartre). Once man is convinced of this, his asking about the meaning of life and the subject's attempt to find a ground for his *existence* enter into their proper dimension. With respect to *this* question and searching, however, Sartre does not give any answer because the possibility of such a question does not even arise in his field of vision. Nevertheless, one could perhaps say that Sartre's implicit doctrine is a "theology without God" (Sciacca).

6. CONCLUSION

"We must often remain silent for lack of holy 'names,' " said Hölderlin in reference to man's efforts to speak of God. Others go further and think that, at least provisionally, we must keep entirely silent about God. But even the Death-of-God theologians cannot execute this "program" and, as long as they continue to speak so loudly and write so much, their firm resolve to keep silent about God remains somewhat ambiguous. It appears impossible to remain silent about God as long as man cannot cease speaking authentically about himself. This authenticity, however, imposes the condition that man does not call "halt" at the very moment when he realizes that he must speak but is unable to use the "simple" word "is" in the way he has always used it hitherto. God *is* not as beings are.

Man, however, is not merely the "saying"-of-"is"-in-the-world, for the "saying-of-"is"-in-the-world which man himself is as an intentional being reveals itself embedded in an "affirmation" whose correlate *is* not but, at the same time, is not *is-not*. This reciprocal implication of "affirmation" and "negation" is the being of man himself as "being over and beyond the world."

In the past, metaphysics in its second phase tried to express this "affirmation" and "negation" on the level of the *cogito*. In Sartre one can find an unwilled attempt to do the same on the level of the *volo*. Heidegger thinks that man must first make a "step back" to find the dimension of his essence in which the Unknown God can disclose Himself to man. "We must often remain silent." At the same time, however, it is certain that man may not let himself be seduced to absolute silence. For anything of which man remains absolutely silent dies for him. But if God had really died for him, modern man would now be in his death agony.

Suggested Readings

Luijpen, *Existential Phenomenology*, Chapter Five. *Phenomenology and Atheism*, Pittsburgh, 2nd impr., 1968, Ch. 2, Sect. 4.

Thomas J. Altizer and William Hamilton, *Radical Theology and the Death of God*, New York, 1966.

A. J. Ayer, *Language, Truth and Logic*, New York, 1948. Many reprints.

John A. Robinson, *Honest to God*, London, 1963.

Heidegger, *Essays in Metaphysics: Identity and Difference*, New York, 1960.

Index of Names

237

INDEX OF NAMES

Index of Subject Matter